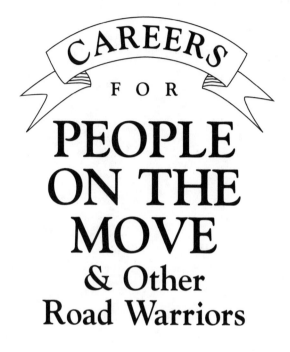

CAREERS

F O R

PEOPLE ON THE MOVE

& Other
Road Warriors

VGM Careers for You Series

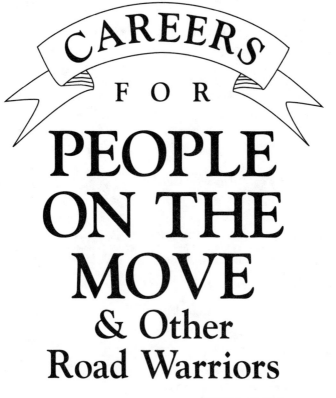

CAREERS

FOR

PEOPLE
ON THE
MOVE

& Other
Road Warriors

Marjorie Eberts
Margaret Gisler

VGM Career Books

*Chicago   New York   San Francisco   Lisbon   London   Madrid   Mexico City
Milan   New Delhi   San Juan   Seoul   Singapore   Sydney   Toronto*

Library of Congress Cataloging-in-Publication Data

Eberts, Marjorie.
   Careers for people on the move & other road warriors / Marjorie Eberts and Margaret Gisler.
      p. cm. — (VGM careers for you series)
     ISBN 0-658-00708-4 (hardcover) — ISBN 0-658-00709-2 (paperback)
     1. Vocational guidance. I. Title: Careers for people on the move and other road warriors. II. Gisler, Margaret. III. Title. IV. Series.

HF5382 .E233   2001
331.7'02—dc21   2001026841

VGM Career Books

A Division of The McGraw·Hill Companies

1 2 3 4 5 6 7 8 9 0   LBM/LBM   0 9 8 7 6 5 4 3 2 1

ISBN: 0-658-00708-4 (hardcover)
      0-658-00709-2 (paperback)

This book was set in Goudy Old Style by ImPrint Services
Printed and bound by Lake Book Manufacturing

McGraw-Hill books are available at special quantity discounts to use as premiums and sales promotions or in corporate training programs. For more information, please write to th Director of Special Sales, Professional Publishing, McGraw-Hill, Two Penn Plaza, New York, NY 10121. Or contact your local bookstore.

This book is printed on acid-free paper.

To the road warriors
in our families who are always
on the move—Marvin,
Martha, Tony, Les, Maria,
Ann, Mark, and David.

Contents

Acknowledgments   ix

CHAPTER ONE
Careers for People on the Move   1

CHAPTER TWO
Careers for Taxi, Van, and Limousine Drivers   11

CHAPTER THREE
Careers for Local Truck Drivers   29

CHAPTER FOUR
Careers for Long-Haul Truck Drivers   49

CHAPTER FIVE
Careers for Bus Drivers   69

CHAPTER SIX
Careers with Delivery Services   91

CHAPTER SEVEN
Careers with Driving Schools   107

CHAPTER EIGHT
More Careers Behind the Wheel   129

APPENDIX A
Checklist for Quality
Truck Driver Training Programs   147

APPENDIX B
Schools for Entry-Level
Truck Driver Training   157

APPENDIX C
Top Fifty Trucking Companies   175

About the Authors   181

Acknowledgments

We wish to thank Kevin Crider for providing substantial help in the researching and writing of this book and Maria Olson for conducting several of the featured interviews.

We also appreciate the help of the following people and organizations that provided valuable information about road warrior jobs and introduced us to many individuals who spend their days on the move.

Matt Croke	BSR, Inc.
Tom Fugee	Transportation Technical Services
Bruce Keplinger	Western Pacific Truck School
Wanda Krug	Educational site manager
Jim Lavrinc	The Driving School Association of the Americas, Inc.
Bob Schauer	Western Pacific Truck School
Jim Sheahan	United Charter Service
Jill Zimmerman	Social worker
Professional Truck Driver Institute	

CHAPTER ONE

Careers for People on the Move

Do you truly enjoy driving? Are you a person who savors every moment behind the wheel? Have people told you that you are a skilled driver who handles city traffic as well as driving on a freeway or a winding mountain road? As a child, did you sit in the family car and pretend to drive for endless hours? Do you like to play video games that test your driving skill? Could "On the Road Again" be your theme song? And do you see yourself as a person who relishes being on the go traveling from one city to another? If so, you are a road warrior who will be happiest working at a job behind the wheel of some type of motor vehicle.

Your ability to drive is an asset that you can use in an amazing variety of careers. Companies are searching for people who want to spend the entire workday in a car, bus, van, or truck.

Is a Career on the Move Right for You?

You know that you like to drive and enjoy being on the move. Is that really enough to embark on a career in which your workplace will be streets, roads, and highways?

Determine whether you have some of the common characteristics of most career road warriors by answering the following questions.

1. Are you safety conscious? Companies want drivers who avoid having accidents.

2. Are you willing to follow safety rules? All jobs on the road require strict adherence to safety regulations.

3. Do you have the stamina to do physically demanding work? Many jobs on the road require considerable lifting.

4. Can you pass a demanding physical examination? Many drivers have to pass a complete physical examination every two years.

5. Are you willing to drive in such adverse conditions as rain, sleet, and icy roads? Many driving jobs regularly present these challenges.

6. Are you patient? Many days will be spent in traffic jams.

7. Are you flexible? Many jobs require you to handle a variety of responsibilities.

8. Can you handle stress? Other drivers on the road may not follow safety rules and may even display road rage.

9. Are you able to work alone? In many driving jobs, you will be the only person in the vehicle.

10. Are you willing to work different shifts? This is often a requirement. You may have to drive at night.

11. Are you willing to get additional training? Many driving jobs require special training and/or continuous education.

12. Do you have solid communication skills? Taxi and bus drivers spend considerable time interacting with riders.

13. Can you work effectively without direct supervision? Drivers usually only have contact with their supervisors by radio.

14. Are you willing to spend days or weeks away from your home? Both long-haul truckers and traveling salespeople are not home every night.

15. Are you comfortable with technology? Driving jobs now involve the use of computers and other high-tech equipment.

A Brief Look at Jobs for People on the Move

When you start looking for jobs that offer the opportunity to spend your days on the road, a large number of possibilities will emerge. You'll find jobs that will let you drive around your community, through out your state, or across the country. You could be transporting people or goods in these jobs or traveling from place to place selling a product or service. The next time you are driving down the road, look at your fellow drivers to see what some of their jobs are. You may see someone driving a tanker truck filled with milk, a busload of commuters, a van with senior citizens, or a school bus. There is just the right job out there for people who want to spend their workdays on the road.

Look at the following want ads. All of these jobs are for road warriors like you. Note that there are both part-time and full-time jobs and that many offer good salaries and benefits.

Route Salesperson: Full-time route salesperson wanted for wholesale distribution. Established route, calling on retail accounts in greater Los Angeles area, selling snacks and food. Some cold calling. Prior sales experience is a must. Must have your own reliable transportation.

Driving Teacher: Small accredited driving school in Detroit. We're growing and seeking driver education teachers for on-the-road training of teens. Will train right person. Top salary and benefits.

Part-Time Truck Driver: Major newspaper is seeking a part-time driver to join our delivery team. Previous driving experience is preferred. Must be able to drive a five-speed manual transmission, twenty-four-foot truck. Requires a regular Class C license and clean driving report. Need to be able to follow directions, read a computer manifest, and lift bundles weighing thirty-five pounds.

Chauffeurs: Knowledge of Miami area. Must be twenty-five years old. Need chauffeur's license. Salary and benefits.

Drivers for Courier Company: Willing to train. Guaranteed base pay and earning potential up to $700 to $1,000 a week. Excellent benefits and 401(k).

Bus Driver: Open routes in the Raleigh-Durham area. Drivers are responsible for keeping special education students comfortable and safe during the trip to and from school. Work is part-time (morning and afternoon), year-round. Benefits available.

Drivers: Be home daily. Drivers average in excess of $50,000 annually delivering gas/diesel around the Chicago area. Must be twenty-five years old with Class A license and one year driving experience.

This book is designed to help road warriors who want to be paid for driving find the perfect job. Here is a glimpse of some of the jobs that you will read about in this book.

Careers for Taxi, Van, and Limousine Drivers

Whenever people want a ride to a destination within a large city or suburb or to the airport, they call upon taxi, van, and limousine drivers to perform this vital service. If you have the skill to locate little-known streets, and you have a good driving record and an excellent sense of direction, you have the basic skills needed for this career. Of course, it also helps if you truly enjoy people, for each trip will bring you in touch with different personalities, from frenzied parents taking a child to the hospital emergency room to tourists eager to sample the cuisine of a well-known restaurant. You may even find yourself driving celebrities, from screen stars to sports figures. This career will also give you the opportunity to choose between working for a company or owning and operating your own vehicle. No matter which of these choices you make, the key to financial success in this career lies in the number of individuals you drive to their destinations each day.

Careers for Local Truck Drivers

Almost every product purchased in stores, service stations, and restaurants traveled at least part of the way on a truck. And, frequently, the final delivery of the product was made by a local truck driver. One of the special benefits of choosing a career as a local truck driver is that you will be able to come home each day. Plus, you will have the opportunity to drive a wide range of vehicles, from eighteen-wheelers to pickup trucks. You can also drive very specialized trucks, such as dry-bulk carriers and tank trucks. No matter what type of truck you drive, you will be involved in some way in the loading and unloading of the truck, even if it is only to direct helpers. Your days can be set if you drive a fixed route to make prearranged deliveries or pick up products. Or every day can mean driving to different locations. If you have a special talent for sales, you can not only drive a truck locally but also sell the product you are carrying.

Careers for Long-Haul Truck Drivers

Long-haul or over-the-road truck drivers lead a very different life from those in most careers—even local drivers. They are typically away from their homes for a week or more, and then the drivers spend just a few days at home before going out on the road again. For some long-haul drivers, their trucks become their only residences, and they live full-time in their comfortable cabs. Some companies use two drivers on very long runs. One drives while the other sleeps, and stops are only made for fuel, food, showers, loading, and unloading. Many of these driver teams are husband and wife. While some long-haul drivers follow the same route on every trip, most go where they are sent by dispatchers to pick up and drop off all kinds of freight. When these drivers start a trip, they rarely know the places they will go or how long they will be gone. The lure of the open road and the camaraderie of fellow truck drivers make this career attractive to long-haul drivers.

Careers for Bus Drivers

Choosing a career as a bus driver involves having far more than good driving skills—you must be able to deal with passengers. If you drive a local or intercity bus, you can expect to collect fares, announce stops, and answer all kinds of questions, including the perennial "When will we get there?" As a school bus driver, you must make sure that all the students are sitting in their seats, treating each other with respect, and entering and exiting the bus in a safe manner. Motor coach drivers who take people on charter and sight-seeing trips have to follow closely the planned schedule as well as work with tour guides to make the trip comfortable for all the passengers. Besides keeping all the passengers happy, bus drivers must often deal with very heavy traffic, so this can be a very stressful job.

Careers with Delivery Services

Everyone wants their letters, packages, and products delivered quickly. Being able to do this is one of the requirements for a successful career with the post office or a delivery service. Besides being a skilled driver, you will need to know every street on your route or service area and be an efficient sorter who can arrange everything that you are delivering in the order that it will be delivered. Just a few years ago, most letters and packages were delivered to homes and businesses by the postal service. While the postal service remains the largest delivery service in the United States, giant companies like FedEx, UPS, and DHL Worldwide Express are now delivering mail and packages at what must seem like "warp" speed. Within most large cities, there are also jobs for couriers, who pick up and deliver letters, important business documents, and packages within as short a time as an hour.

Careers with Driving Schools

All road warriors and people constantly on the move in motor vehicles need to become safe, skilled drivers. The individuals who help them achieve this goal are the instructors in driving schools. Most of these jobs are at driving schools teaching beginning drivers the secrets of parallel parking, entering and exiting freeways, and just driving safely. You don't have to have nerves of steel for this job, but you do have to be a very skilled driver with a knack for teaching, especially working with teenagers. Truckers driving the large tractor-trailers as well as bigger straight trucks are required by federal law to get a commercial driver's license. Truck driving schools have programs that help them earn this license and get the training in driving these big rigs that both trucking and insurance companies want their drivers to have. Some instructors spend all their time on the job in behind-the-wheel training of future truckers. Others will spend part of their time in the classroom. For the extremely skilled driver, there is also the possibility of teaching racing techniques, stunt driving, and high-performance driving at driving schools such as the Bob Bondurant School.

More Careers Behind the Wheel

Many other careers offer you the opportunity to be on the move for most of the workday in a car or truck. These careers, however, may not be thought of as driving careers. For example, many state, county, and local police officers spend almost all of their hours on the job in patrol cars making sure that traffic laws are followed. Quite often, these officers have had specialized training to enable them to handle their vehicles when they are involved in chases. Another career that will put you behind the wheel for most of your working day is that of traveling salesperson. Then the car often becomes your only office, with a computer, telephone, and file cases. And many firefighters and emergency medical technicians spend considerable time behind the wheel every day and need to be very skilled drivers. The list of careers that will put you in the driver's seat also includes race car driver, parking lot attendant, heavy-equipment operator, wide-load warning driver, and all the other drivers that you observe doing their jobs as they travel down the road.

What You Need to Become a Road Warrior

Companies will not hire you just because you want to spend your days behind the wheels of a motor vehicle. They will expect you to demonstrate solid driving skills as well as other skills that are essential to excelling at a driving job. For most of these jobs, an ability to handle paperwork efficiently is necessary. Some jobs require excellent communication skills.

Most driving jobs only require graduation from high school or the equivalent. However, you will have to obtain special licenses to work at many of these jobs. This can be done most easily by attending a driving school.

The better you can drive, read maps, handle paperwork, and use a computer, the better you will be prepared for a driving career. Those of you who land the very best jobs will often have had some previous work experience.

Finding Your Dream Job

There is always a demand for drivers, and there are even tremendous shortages of drivers in some career areas, especially truck driving. If you have the needed skills, you should not find it too difficult to get a job. While your first job may not be your dream job, it should lead to the job that you want as you gain valuable experience.

The traditional ways of obtaining jobs work well for drivers. Read the want ads in your local newspapers and contact the companies where you may wish to work. You can also get leads from friends who have driving jobs. Visit state employment offices, too. And in today's Internet world, many jobs can be found by visiting company websites, as well as sites that list all kinds of jobs.

CHAPTER TWO

Careers for Taxi, Van, and Limousine Drivers

Not everyone has a car to use all the time. And buses don't always follow routes that will take people to their planned destinations. Fortunately, there are taxicabs, limousines, and vans to help people be mobile both day and night. Some huge cities, like New York and Chicago, will actually have more taxis, limousines, and vans on certain streets in their business districts during rush hour than cars.

Most taxis, vans, and limousines are found in metropolitan areas, although even small towns are likely to have companies offering some personal transportation service. These vehicles transport people to work, airports, hotels, and such leisure activities as movies, dinner, and shopping. They take celebrities to the Oscars, baseball fans to games, senior citizens to medical appointments, and executives to meetings across town. If you want to meet new people every day and drive them to their destinations, being a taxi, van, or limousine driver may be the career on the move that is right for you.

The Beginnings of Taxicabs

Throughout history, people have been in the business of transporting individuals from one place to another. At first, they actually carried them. Remember the movie scenes of Cleopatra entering Rome? From the earliest of times, drivers have also transported individuals in horse-drawn vehicles. It was not, however, until the late 1800s that a motorized vehicle was used in Paris, France. In the United States, taxicabs first appeared in about 1898. Then, during World War I, taxicabs were used for a very unusual reason: the French used them to transport troops from Paris to the Marne River battlefield. Today, taxicabs are used throughout the world.

The word *taxicab* actually comes from combining and shortening the words *taximeter* and *cabriolet*. The taximeter was a device invented by Wilhelm Bruhn to accurately calculate the distance traveled and the resulting fare. The cabriolet was a two-wheeled, horse-drawn carriage often used for hire. Most modern taxicabs are still using taximeters to determine fares.

What It's Like to Drive a Taxicab

Taxi drivers or cab drivers usually drive around the streets looking for people who need a ride. Passengers hail or "wave down" drivers as they cruise through the streets. This is how taxi drivers get most of their customers. Drivers may also have prearranged pickups in which passengers call the taxi company, give their location, and ask to be picked up at a certain time. The taxi company dispatcher then calls the driver on a radio, cellular phone, or onboard computer to inform the driver about the pick-up. Many larger cities have established taxi stands where passengers can wait for a taxi. These taxi stands are commonly located at places where people frequently need a taxi, such as airports, hotels, and train stations.

As a taxi driver, you would probably drive a large four-door car that has been converted for passenger transport. Some taxis are specially equipped to transport disabled passengers or the elderly. These drivers get special training to operate the equipment safely and transport special-needs passengers.

Basic Duties

Once they pick up a passenger, drivers will turn on the taximeter to start determining what the fare will be. Sometimes, they will need to load luggage or packages for the passenger. When the traffic is heavy or the weather is bad, taxi drivers must be extremely careful not to have or cause an accident. Plus, they have to avoid sudden stops or turns that might jar their passengers. It is absolutely essential for cab drivers to be familiar with city streets so they can get the passengers to their destinations quickly. They also must know how to get to commonly requested destinations, such as hotels, convention centers, railroad stations, and airports. Plus, they should be prepared to give recommendations on places to visit and good restaurants. Taxi drivers also need to know the location of hospitals and fire and police stations in case of a passenger emergency.

Once a driver reaches a passenger's destination, he or she must calculate the fare and inform the passenger. Fares often have many parts. The taximeter measures the fare based on the length and the amount of time the trip took. There may be an added charge for additional passengers, a fee for handling luggage, or a drop charge—an additional flat fee added for the use of the cab. Passengers usually add a tip or gratuity to the fare. The tip is based on how satisfied the passenger is with the driver's service. Then the driver logs all information about the trip on the trip sheet. This information includes where and when the passenger was picked up, the destination, and the total fee for the trip. It is also a record for the taxi company of the driver's activity and efficiency.

Work Conditions

As a taxi driver, your work hours can vary a great deal. Some drivers work full-time with regular hours. Part-time drivers will likely have work hours that can change from day to day. It isn't unusual for taxi drivers to be called to work on short notice. Full-time taxi drivers usually work one eight- to twelve-hour shift per day. Part-time drivers work half a shift each day, or a full shift one or two times per week. Many taxi companies offer service twenty-four hours a day, so drivers need to be on duty day and night. Early morning and late evening shifts are common. Taxi drivers may need to work long shifts during holidays, weekends, or other special events to meet increased demand for taxi service. Traditionally, New Year's Eve is the busiest night of the year. And the busiest times each day are likely to be when the traffic is most congested. Independent drivers are able to set their own hours and schedules.

Being a taxi driver is a very sedentary job, as most road warrior jobs are. However, it is not a solitary job; you will be in the position of spending your time on the job dealing with people. The more successful you are, the more people you will drive each day. You will encounter people with friendly and antagonistic personalities and those who are in a hurry as well as relaxed. From fare to fare, you will be adjusting to the different demands of your passengers. You will also be in an enclosed space with those wearing too much cologne and some who are inebriated.

Qualifications and Training

You cannot work as a taxi driver without the appropriate licenses. Local governments set the license requirements for taxi drivers, so they can vary from city to city. Minimum requirements include having a regular automobile driver's license. It is also necessary to get a chauffeur or taxi driver's license. This usually requires the driver to pass a written exam or complete a training program. Applicants must know motor vehicle laws, safe driving practices, local geography, taxicab regulations, and show some aptitude for customer service.

Since taxi drivers have to deal with all kinds of people, you will need to be tolerant and patient even when a customer is rude to handle this job. Having patience is also important when you are driving in heavy traffic. Because passengers rely on taxi drivers to pick them up on time and get them to their destination quickly, you must be dependable. And you also should like to talk to strangers if you elect to become a taxi driver, because there is a lot of talking in this job.

Taxi drivers need to be expert drivers with good driving records. Some taxicab companies offer on-the-job training for their new drivers. They show them how to use the taximeter and communication equipment and how to complete paperwork. New drivers will learn about popular sight-seeing and entertainment destinations as well as driver safety.

Most taxi drivers pay a fee to a cab company to lease their vehicles. Some buy their own taxis and go into business for themselves. These independent owner-drivers need a special permit to operate their vehicles as a company. An independent driver needs to have good business sense and be responsible as well as self-motivated to be successful. Taking courses in accounting and business can be quite helpful. Knowing how to perform routine maintenance and make repairs can reduce expenses.

Job Outlook and Earnings

There are usually good opportunities to get a job as a taxi driver because many drivers transfer to other occupations or leave the labor force. Opportunities are best for those who have good driving records and are willing to work flexible schedules. You will find the most job openings in metropolitan areas that are experiencing rapid population growth. The number of job openings does fluctuate from month to month and season to season. Extra drivers are frequently hired during holiday and high tourist seasons.

How much you earn as a taxi driver depends so much on the hours you work, the tips you make, and where you work. Not counting tips, the earnings of taxi drivers vary from less than $6 per hour to more than $12 per hour. Owner-drivers earn from $20,000 to $30,000 per year, including tips. In large metropolitan areas, earnings are usually higher.

Driving a Taxi in the City

Jason Pace has been driving a taxi in a suburban community for several years. He got his job because he was a friend of the company owner's son. He first began driving part-time and later, with more experience, started working full-time. Jason drives a minivan rather than the typical car most taxi drivers use. Before he could begin driving a taxi, he had to get a special permit from the city. While this is no longer the case in his state, new drivers do need to be fingerprinted and have a good driving record.

In this job, Jason believes it is helpful to be a good listener and a "mini-psychiatrist." It is not unusual for people to share their life histories and all their troubles with him in a fifteen-minute taxi ride. Having a good sense of humor is helpful, too. Jason feels good taxi drivers need to have an even temperament and lots of patience, especially when driving in heavy traffic.

A Typical Day for Jason

Jason begins his day at about 8:00 A.M. when he turns on his radio in order to get calls from the dispatcher. The taxi is his office, so Jason leaves his radio on all day. He is usually very busy in the morning because he transports many commuters. When Jason first began driving, the heavy traffic during the morning and afternoon commutes really stressed him out. But as he became more experienced, he gained confidence and was able to focus more on customer service and being courteous to his passenger. Because he works on commission and for tips, it is important for him to be efficient, friendly, and helpful with his passengers.

Jason has fewer riders during the late morning and early afternoon. Then he gets busy again as commuters end their workdays and need transportation home. During his day, Jason may make several long hauls to the local airport. Occasionally, he delivers packages for people or companies. His day ends between 4:00 and 5:00 P.M.

Career Pluses and Minuses

Jason likes driving a taxi because each day is different. It's never routine. Some days he will work on the west side of town. Other days he works all over town, or he makes runs to the airport. He doesn't see the same people day after day, although he does have a few regular customers he enjoys transporting. Jason also gets the opportunity to help a lot of elderly passengers, which makes him feel good. Another big plus for Jason is that he earns a very good income driving a taxi.

One negative to this job, according to Jason, is not receiving any benefits. Also, he is displeased that people do not highly regard taxi driving as a career. In addition, he points out there is little opportunity for advancement. And, of course, heavy traffic can be a big problem some days.

The most negative aspect of this job is the risk of robbery. Jason drives only during the day, and his route covers a suburban area, so his risk is not as great as for some other drivers. Nevertheless, he still is very cautious.

Driving a Taxi for Special-Needs Passengers

Brandon Lockhart drives a taxi for a company that transports people with disabilities and the elderly. He has been driving for this company for five and a half years. His vehicle is a full-size extended van with a high roof. It is equipped with a wheelchair lift, although not all of the company's vans include lifts. Brandon's van has four high-backed seats fitted with shoulder and lap belts and room for two wheelchairs.

A typical day for Brandon begins at 7:00 A.M., when he picks up his route sheet, which includes scheduled pickups and drop-offs. Next, he goes to the garage area to get his assigned van. He usually has the same van from day to day. The company does have a maintenance crew, but Brandon still likes to check over the van before beginning his day. He always checks the lights, flashers, oil, tires, and fuel. If he sees anything is wrong, he reports it to the maintenance crew to be fixed. Very rarely does he find any problems because the overnight crew is thorough and has the van ready for him first thing in the morning. Once he has checked everything on the van, it is time for him to get rolling.

Brandon's First Passenger

Brandon has to pick up an elderly woman who has a doctor's appointment at a local hospital. When he arrives at the woman's house, he goes to the door to announce his arrival. Sometimes, he helps passengers put on their coats or carries things for them. He often has to assist them as they climb the three small steps to enter the van. Some of the passengers have a difficult time fastening their seat belts, so Brandon offers his assistance. Once today's first passenger is safely buckled in, he can continue to his next stop, where he is picking up another person before stopping at the hospital.

Brandon's Second Stop

This stop is at an apartment complex with many little lanes interconnecting the buildings. Brandon says complexes like this and subdivisions can be tricky to drive through and sometimes even trickier when it comes to finding the right apartment or home. In one part of this city, the area is growing rapidly and there are many new streets that aren't even on maps yet. In cases like this, Brandon has to call the taxi office on his cell phone or call the passenger for exact directions. This passenger at the second stop regularly uses his taxi so Brandon knows exactly where to go. Again, he helps the passenger get on the van and get buckled into the seat. Next stop, the hospital.

At the Hospital

Brandon helps his two passengers exit the van and enter the hospital. Sometimes, he will help passengers find out where they need to go for their appointments. Since Brandon regularly takes passengers to the hospital, he knows his way around quite well. Depending on his schedule, Brandon may wait at the hospital for one of his passengers. At times, he will pick up someone already at the hospital who is waiting for a ride. On other occasions, it is back on the road to his next scheduled pickup. Today, his dispatcher has called to give him an address for a pickup that has just called for a ride. The dispatcher knows Brandon is closest to this address because each van is equipped with a tracking device. The device shows Brandon's exact location on a computer in the dispatcher's office. So it's off to his next stop.

A Closer Look at Brandon's Job

Brandon's days are usually busy. He also has days when he and two or three others drivers have very few scheduled stops. They often spend their wait time in the garage area. Since they are on call, they must always be ready to go out on a run. The drivers like sharing stories, taking short naps, and watching some television. Some of the more energetic drivers wash or vacuum their vans. Brandon likes to keep his van looking good because his passengers feel more comfortable in a clean, well-running vehicle. Brandon's day ends between 3:00 and 4:00 P.M. He turns his van into the garage crew, who fuel it up for the next driver who will have it on the road until about 7:00 P.M. This second-shift driver is almost always a part-time employee.

More About Brandon's Job

Brandon first became interested in this job when a family member was temporarily wheelchair bound and needed transportation in a specialty van. He went to the company and applied for a driver position. He had to go through a background check. Then Brandon completed a company-sponsored training program that included getting his chauffeur's license. He also learned basic first aid, CPR, and how to operate the wheelchair lift. He had to demonstrate that he was familiar with the city's streets and the location of the city's three hospitals. At first, Brandon only worked on a call-in basis on the evening shift. Several months later, a position opened up on the day shift that was full-time.

Brandon earns an hourly wage and is not allowed to accept tips, but many people like to give him little gifts to show their appreciation for his services. He also gets health insurance, sick leave, and vacation time through the company. The company is currently investigating the possibility of offering a 401(k) plan for its drivers.

Career Pluses and Minuses

What Brandon likes most about this job is being able to help the elderly and disabled and talking with lots of different people every day. The older people have many great stories to tell to someone willing to listen. Because he is a true road warrior, he especially likes being on the road most of the day. Brandon doesn't like bad weather and especially dislikes the first few snowfalls of the winter. He says this is when drivers forget how to drive carefully. Brandon is a very cautious driver, which has paid off because he has never had an accident in his van. As far as passengers go, he doesn't like having complainers who never know when to stop complaining.

Future Plans

Brandon really likes driving his van. He wants to buy a van and start his own taxi service someday in a small or medium-size city. He would like for the elderly and disabled everywhere to have affordable transportation available to them whenever they need it—just like the people in the town where he now works.

What It's Like to Be a Chauffeur

Chauffeurs drive limousines and stretch limousines, vans and luxury vans, corporate sedans, and private cars. They may drive for limousine companies, government offices, private businesses, or individuals. Many chauffeurs drive large vans between hotels and airports, bus depots, or train stations. Some chauffeurs drive luxury cars or limousines to proms, weddings, and other social events; to conventions and business meetings; or to entertainment events such as movie premieres, theater show openings, and sporting events. Other chauffeurs provide full-time, personal service to the wealthy or to private companies. A few chauffeurs provide protective and antikidnap services. There is also a trend toward having chauffeurs work as full-service executive assistants, acting as drivers, secretaries, and itinerary planners.

Chauffeurs typically provide passengers with a high level of special service. They pay particular attention to opening doors, holding umbrellas when it is raining, and loading or unloading packages from the trunk of the vehicle. They may also deliver packages or pick up clients for their employers. Many chauffeurs provide amenities such as music, television, newspapers, magazines, and telephones that make riding in their limousines enjoyable.

Work Conditions

The needs of clients or an employer dictate the work hours of chauffeurs, so their hours can change from day to day. They must expect to spend considerable time waiting for their passengers. For example, they may pick newlyweds up and take them to the reception and then wait until the reception ends to take them to the airport. Or a personal chauffeur may take his employer to work, wait, drive the employer to a meeting, wait, return the employer to the office, wait, and then drive the employer home. Chauffeurs commonly must work evenings and weekends and may be on call all day long. Chauffeurs who work for hotels, resorts, and companies typically have regular hours; however, they can expect to work shifts.

Like taxi drivers, chauffeurs transport a variety of people, from rock stars to high school students going to a prom, and must provide the appropriate level of service the passengers require. On the job, they will usually be far more formally dressed than taxi drivers. Chauffeurs for businesspeople typically wear suits or even a uniform. Those who are driving passengers to special events may even wear tuxedos. Chauffeurs driving shuttle vehicles may only need to wear neat and clean clothes.

Qualifications and Training

Many limousine companies have requirements for their drivers that exceed the standards and requirements put in place by local governments. These companies often have higher minimum age requirements and look for drivers with a high school diploma. They may also conduct an investigation into the driver's medical, credit, criminal, and driving records. In addition, companies look for drivers who are friendly and courteous and able to relate well to a wide variety of passengers.

In order to become a chauffeur, you will need to hold a regular driver's license and obtain a chauffeur's license by passing a written test or completing a chauffeur's training course. The test typically includes motor vehicle laws, safe driving practices, and regulations concerning chauffeuring. Some companies provide new drivers with on-the-job training, which may include learning to operate the vehicle's communication equipment and how to provide superior customer service. A company may require their drivers to complete reports after each driving job or at the end of their shifts.

Job Outlook and Earnings

Employment opportunities for chauffeurs will continue to grow, especially in metropolitan areas. Chauffeurs who work for limousine companies typically are paid by the hour and may have some benefits. They will also receive tips. The amount will depend on the level of service provided as well as the personal inclinations of the passenger. Drivers who work for businesses and individuals are usually salaried. Some chauffeurs own and operate their own vehicles and may work independently or offer their services to a variety of employers. Chauffeurs who work full-time can earn from $25,000 to $60,000 a year.

Working for a Large Limousine Company

Craig Butler works as a chauffeur and limousine driver. He has a degree in education, has been a teacher, and has worked in construction. When he needed additional income, Craig started working evenings as a chauffeur. This required him to get a chauffeur's license.

For about four years, Craig drove part-time for the state of Indiana before deciding to become a full-time limousine driver. He now drives for Carey Indiana, which is part of Carey International based in Washington, D.C. This company is one of the largest chauffeur limousine services in the country and has branches all over the United States from coast to coast. Carey Indiana contracts with companies in the area to provide drivers for executives, transportation to special events, and airport pickup services.

Besides driving limousines, Craig drives Lincoln Town Cars and vans, as not all of the company's customers wish to use limousines. Craig usually works twelve hours or more a day about five days a week. Most of the company chauffeurs work one of the weekend evenings. Because of his seniority, Craig doesn't have to work weekends. He works days, and most of his passengers are businesspeople or professionals.

Working with Passengers

Craig frequently does airport runs as well as taking passengers to parties and concerts. Often, the passengers will have extra tickets that they give to him. When the company had a contract with a local radio station to chauffeur entertainers who were in the city to perform concerts, he received some backstage passes to the concerts.

People often asked Craig if he has driven anyone famous. He has chauffeured Gina Lee Noland, who is Neely on the television show "Baywatch." He drove Gina and her husband to a local hockey game, where she threw out a puck. He has also driven for Larry King, Chris Weber from the Sacramento Kings, and Olympic gymnastics gold medalist Shannon Miller, who gave him an eight-by-ten picture of herself.

When Craig is driving businesspeople, he works hard at getting them to relax. He has noticed that people who fly into the airport are often stressed when they get into his car. Craig tries to get them to talk to help relieve some of the stress. However, he points out that it is important in this job to know when passengers want to talk and when they want to be left alone. One key signal for stopping any conversation efforts is seeing passengers take out their laptop computers. Meeting the client's needs ensures that Craig will receive a good tip.

The Financial Side of the Job

The chauffeurs at the limousine company are paid an hourly wage. Tips belong entirely to the driver and are not shared with the company. Craig pays for his own uniform and cell phone, while the company supplies the car.

Craig chose to work at Carey because the size of the company presents certain advantages. Since Carey is a nationwide company, the greater volume translates into greater earnings for Craig and the other drivers. Drivers who are willing to work more hours or work late into the night—to 2:00 or 3:00 A.M.—can earn more.

Career Pluses and Minuses

Craig likes working as a chauffeur because he is able to earn a good income while being on the move throughout his workday. He also likes to meet and talk to the people who come from all over the world.

Because he is a true road warrior, he likes the fact that he doesn't have to sit behind a desk every day. Craig enjoys the freedom this job offers. No boss is looking over his shoulder. While he sometimes has to deal with difficult passengers, Craig has learned ways to deal with them effectively and does not let them bother him.

Career Advice

Craig advises those who are just starting out as chauffeurs not to worry about the low income they are likely to earn at first. He knows that with experience, new drivers will learn how to work with their passengers. Then the supervisors will notice their increasing expertise and begin to give them better job assignments, which will lead to better tips.

Driving a Hotel Shuttle Van

Salvador Bell drives a shuttle van for a hotel in Fort Wayne, Indiana. He also helps at the front desk and with the bellhop's duties between his driving runs. The shuttle he drives is a full-size van. Each seat is high backed and well padded for passenger comfort. Most of Salvador's runs are to the airport to pick up hotel guests who fly into the city for visits or business.

After graduating from high school in Mexico City, he came to the United States and began attending college and working. Salvador became interested in the hotel job because it offered the flexible hours he needed in order to attend an academy to become a certified travel agent and because it would give him valuable experience in the travel industry.

To be able to drive the hotel's shuttle van, Salvador had to earn his chauffeur's license. The local branch of the state's Bureau of Motor Vehicles gave Salvador the materials he needed to study in order to pass the written examination for the license. Salvador had to learn the rules of the road, regulations for chauffeurs, and special rules for drivers when they are transporting passengers. Salvador's license allows him to drive vehicles that carry fewer than fifteen passengers.

On the Road with Salvador

Before Salvador goes out on the road, he performs a pretrip check of the shuttle. He checks the oil, tires, lights, and windshield wipers. He also checks to see that the shuttle is clean inside and out. Then, just before he pulls out, he checks his mirrors for proper alignment.

When hotel guests make reservations, they may ask to be picked up at the airport when they arrive. Other guests will call from the airport and ask for shuttle service to the hotel. When Salvador travels to the airport to pick up or drop off guests, he must park in a designated location in order to avoid getting a parking ticket. If he is picking up passengers, he will frequently have to look for them. This may require checking the flight monitors in the airport to see if a flight is delayed and, if so, for how long.

As soon as Salvador greets passengers, he helps them with their luggage and will load it into the van. Most of the people who ride in the shuttle are very interesting, friendly people. Salvador knows the importance of being courteous to the guests. One thing he really likes about this job is the opportunity to meet people from all over the world. Driving them around gives him the chance to learn about other countries.

Salvador's job is not limited to airport runs; he also transports people to other places throughout the city. In order to do this, he has become familiar with the city's streets, popular attractions, and local malls. Passengers frequently ask him which restaurants are good, what movies are playing, or what special events are taking place. Keeping up-to-date about what is going on in the city is essential for this shuttle van driver.

A Challenging Situation

Driving the hotel shuttle bus can sometimes be a challenge. Salvador often has passengers who have limited English skills. Communicating with them can be quite difficult. He remembers one incident in which a hotel guest from the Far East asked to be taken to a meeting at an industrial plant that was located well beyond the shuttle's twelve-mile travel limit. The guest couldn't understand why Salvador could not drive him to his meeting. The hotel management was finally able to help the guest understand and did get the guest a taxi so he could get to his meeting.

For More Information

To learn more about licensing requirements for employment as a taxi driver or chauffeur, contact the offices of local government agencies regulating taxicabs. To find out about job opportunities, contact local taxicab or limousine companies or state employment service offices. For the special firsthand knowledge of what is involved in a career driving a taxi, van, or limousine, talk to people who actually have these jobs.

If you want general information about the work of taxi drivers and the taxi industry, contact:

International Taxicab and Livery Association
3849 Farragut Avenue
Kensington, MD 20895
www.taxinetwork.com

For general information about the work of limousine drivers, contact:

National Limousine Association
900 North Pitt Street, Suite 220
Alexandria, VA 22314

CHAPTER THREE

Careers for Local Truck Drivers

The United States moves by truck. Wherever there is a road, you'll see trucks moving goods: food, clothing, gasoline, cars, lumber, furniture, appliances, and just about every product that you use in your daily life. Because of their ability to link up with ships, trains, and airplanes, trucks usually make the initial pickup and final delivery of goods. Trucks actually carry nearly all goods at some point in their journey from producer to consumer.

Trucks range in size from local delivery vans bringing flowers, cleaning, and furniture to your home to the largest tractor-trailers hauling anything from computers to canned food across the country. Each and every truck on the road presents a career opportunity for some driver, and that person on the move could possibly be you.

The Development of the Trucking Industry

One of the most important factors in the development of the trucking industry has been the desire of people to trade. While they weren't using trucks, but carts, people who lived in what is now Europe were already moving such things as salt, flint, lead, and tin throughout the area more than four thousand years ago. Even when goods were transported by water, carts were still needed to bring them closer to people. The need for local transport continued after trains began to carry freight in the early 1800s.

It was not until about one hundred years ago that trucks came on the scene and began to carry freight. The very first truck was built by Gottlieb Daimler of Germany in 1896. It had a four-horsepower engine and two speeds forward and one in reverse. Two years later, the Winton Company in the United States built a delivery truck with a single-cylinder, six-horsepower engine. These early trucks with their solid-rubber tires and primitive springs were driven over such poor roads that they gave the first truck drivers an incredibly rough ride. In fact, many of these trucks literally shook themselves apart. Nevertheless, they could move faster than the horse-drawn vehicles that had been used to carry goods. They weren't, however, able to carry very heavy loads. Often, the truck was heavier than the load it could carry. Nevertheless, in 1904, there were seven hundred trucks delivering goods locally in the United States. Longer hauls were done by boat or train.

By World War I, there were approximately 250,000 trucks in the United States, and they had become bigger, faster, and more durable. Trucks had really shown how necessary they were when railroads were not able to move all the war supplies to the East Coast for shipment to Europe. Convoys of trucks aided in this job. They had to follow very circuitous routes to find good roads and adequate bridges. This mass movement of goods was the beginning of intercity trucking.

Types of Trucks

As you have probably observed while driving down the road, trucks come in all sizes, from step-up vans to truck-tractors drawing one or more trailers. By government regulation, trucks are typically classified by gross weight. Light trucks, which include vans and small pickups, weigh up to fourteen thousand pounds. Most trucks on the road fall into this category. Medium trucks weigh from fourteen thousand to thirty-three thousand pounds. These trucks usually have all axles attached to a single frame. Heavy trucks weigh more than thirty-three thousand pounds and are the tractor-trailers that make most long-distance hauls. There are also specialty trucks such as tankers, moving vans, lumber trucks, fire engines, concrete mixers, refrigerator trucks, and dry-bulk carriers. During their careers as truck drivers, most will drive more than one type of vehicle.

Career Opportunities in Truck Driving

When it comes to a career driving a truck, many options exist for you. You could work for a food, car, or furniture store that hauls only its own products or for a carrier that serves many shippers and receivers. In either case, the basic decision that you will have to make in this career is whether you wish to be a local or short-haul driver or a long-haul driver, also known as an over-the-road driver. The major difference is that local truck drivers are assigned short runs that can usually be completed in a day, while long-haul drivers may be on the road for a week or more. Another difference is that local truck drivers drive all types of trucks, and long-haul drivers usually drive tractor-trailer trucks. In this chapter, the work of local truck drivers will be explored in detail, while Chapter 4 will describe the careers of long-haul drivers.

The Many Tasks of Local Truck Drivers

No matter what type of goods local drivers haul, they generally return to home base the same day. Some drivers never leave a city, while others may travel between several nearby cities. Drivers may have the same assignment every day, following a specific route. Others may make local deliveries or pickups that vary from day to day. And a few drivers may also have sales responsibilities. The work that individual drivers do depends on the products that they transport. For example, produce truckers usually pick up loaded trucks early in the morning and spend the rest of the day delivering produce to many different grocery stores. On the other hand, a lumber truck driver would make several trips from the lumberyard to one or more construction sites. Gasoline tank truck drivers pick up gas at a refinery and then deliver it to numerous gas stations in the course of a day.

A Typical Day for Most Local Truck Drivers

At the start of the workday, when local drivers leave the terminal or warehouse, they check their trucks for fuel and oil. They also inspect the trucks to make sure the brakes, windshield wipers, and lights are working and that a fire extinguisher, flares, and other safety equipment are aboard and in working condition. In addition, they have the responsibility of making sure the cargo is secure.

Typically, before the drivers arrive, material handlers have loaded the trucks and arranged the items in order of delivery to minimize handling of the goods. Drivers also need to adjust their mirrors so that both sides of the truck are visible from the driver's seat. Many companies require their drivers to follow a checklist to ensure that every safety step is followed. At the end of their inspection, drivers report the equipment that does not work or is missing to the dispatcher.

Before drivers begin their runs, they are given paperwork detailing their stops and what will be delivered and/or picked up at each stop. If they do not drive a regular route, the drivers choose the order of their stops and arrange the paperwork accordingly. At each stop, customers must sign receipts for the goods received or placed on the truck. They must also pay the drivers the balance due on the merchandise if there is a cash-on-delivery arrangement. Drivers try to deliver goods as fast as possible at each stop. This is often difficult because they may have to get in line behind other drivers who are also delivering goods. At the end of the workday, drivers return to the home base and turn in receipts, money, records of deliveries made, and any reports on mechanical problems with their trucks.

The Tasks of Driver-Sales Workers

Besides having all the responsibilities of local truck drivers, driver-sales workers perform many additional tasks at each stop and may use their selling abilities to increase sales and gain additional customers for their companies' products. This is a good job for drivers who want a greater variety of responsibilities.

Most of these drivers have wholesale routes delivering to businesses and stores rather than homes. You have probably seen some of these drivers in grocery stores arranging bread, cakes, rolls, and other baked goods on display racks. Bakery driver-sales workers will also estimate the amount and variety of baked goods to stock by paying close attention to the items that sell well and those sitting on the shelves. They may recommend changes in a store's order or may encourage the manager to stock new bakery products.

Drivers who service vending machines in factories, schools, and other buildings are another example of driver-sales workers. They check items remaining in the machines, replace stock, and remove money deposited in the cash boxes. They also examine each vending machine to make minor repairs, clean machines, and see that merchandise and change are being dispensed properly. After they have completed their routes, driver-sales workers order items for their next delivery based on what products have been selling well, the weather, time of year, and any customer feedback.

Work Conditions for Local Truck Drivers

Every year, it becomes easier in many ways to be a truck driver. Trucks now ride more comfortably, paperwork is handled more efficiently, and traffic and weather reports are more accurate. Nevertheless, driving a truck is physically demanding. Drivers are often required to unload goods at each stop. Some of this cargo, such as doors, mattresses, and office equipment, can be quite heavy. In fact, it may be so heavy that a helper rides with the driver to assist in lifting the cargo. Besides physical demands, driving a truck can be stressful. Traffic is very congested in many cities and on highways, and drivers may often just creep along in traffic with cars frequently cutting in front of them. When you are on the move all day in a truck, you quickly learn that not all drivers obey traffic laws. Plus, because it takes trucks so much longer to stop, you must anticipate what is going to happen next on the road far more than the driver of a passenger vehicle. In addition, you must endure hours of driving in the rain or on icy streets. Driving a truck requires concentration on the road at all times.

Days for local truck drivers can be long in order for them to complete all their deliveries. It is not unusual for drivers to work thirteen- to fifteen-hour days. Not all of these hours will be spent behind the wheel, for state and federal laws usually limit this time to ten hours a day. The remainder of the time is typically spent waiting to get your truck loaded or unloaded. Driving a truck is not necessarily a nine-to-five job. Many local drivers begin their days as early as 2:00 A.M. This is especially true for those who handle food for chain grocery stores, produce markets, and bakeries. Because some cities have local ordinances that severely limit the number of hours that trucks can be on their streets during the day, local drivers may only be able to make deliveries at night.

In considering a career as a local truck driver, you need to be aware of the fact that your driving skill will be challenged daily, especially if you are driving a tractor-trailer. You may need to maneuver down alleys where your clearance can be measured in inches—not feet. Plus, the most difficult thing for truck drivers to do is to back up. Unfortunately, local truck drivers have to do more backing up than any other truckers.

Job Qualifications and Training

State regulations govern the qualifications and standards for local truck drivers. However, drivers of hazardous materials and those who cross states lines must also comply with federal regulations. In addition to these regulations, many companies have their own standards that may be higher than state and federal standards. You can also expect your employer to require a clean driving record.

Licensing

All local truck drivers must have a state driver's license. A regular driver's license is often sufficient to drive light trucks and vans and will also enable you to drive within the borders of many states when you are only eighteen. If you will be driving a vehicle that is designed to carry at least twenty-six thousand pounds, which includes most tractor-trailers as well as bigger straight trucks, you will need a commercial driver's license (CDL) from the state in which you live. You will also need this license to operate trucks transporting hazardous materials and those engaged in interstate commerce no matter what the size of the truck.

To qualify for a commercial driver's license, you will have to be at least twenty-one years old. You will need to pass a written test on rules and regulations and then actually demonstrate that you can operate a commercial truck safely in order to get this license. In addition, the state will check a national data bank to make sure that you have not had a license suspended or revoked in another state. The minimum requirements for this license will be given in Chapter 4, as long-haul drivers must also obtain commercial licenses. You can get information on how to apply for a commercial driver's license from your state's motor vehicle administration.

Training

Taking a driver training course in high school helps in preparing for a future career as a local truck driver, as is taking courses in automotive mechanics. You can also learn on the job, especially if you are driving a light truck or van. Companies prefer to train drivers of tractor-trailers in their own classes or for these drivers to have completed training programs with private or public technical-vocation schools. Study carefully the checklist for finding quality tractor-trailer driver training schools in Appendix A as well as the list of industry-certified courses in schools in Appendix B, as there are schools with courses that do not provide sufficient training or driving time to assure you a job on completion of their programs. Before enrolling in a school, you should also check with local trucking companies to make sure a school's training is acceptable.

Starting Out as a Truck Driver

As a new driver, you can expect to be assigned immediately to a regular driving job; however, some companies may start you out as a truck driver helper. When helpers gain experience and demonstrate their reliability, they receive driving assignments. It is also common to begin as an extra driver substituting for regular drivers who are ill or on vacation. Then, you will get a regular assignment when an opening occurs. New drivers sometimes start on panel or other small trucks and advance to larger and heavier trucks as they gain experience.

As a new driver, you can usually expect some informal training from your employer. It may consist of only a few hours of instruction from an experienced driver, sometimes on your own time. You may also ride with and observe experienced drivers before being assigned your own run. Some companies give one to two days of classroom instruction covering general duties, the operation and loading of a truck, company policies, and the preparation of delivery forms and company records. Plus, your first months as a driver may be made easier because you are assigned an experienced company driver as a mentor to answer your questions and give you advice. Driver-sales workers also receive training on the various types of company products so they will be more effective sales workers and better able to handle customer requests.

Job Outlook

There are more than sixty thousand local trucking companies. Most of these firms primarily carry goods within a metropolitan area and nearby suburbs and nonurban areas. Not all of these companies offer job opportunities; many just have one driver who is also the owner. You are most likely to find a job with a small company because three out of four trucking companies employ fewer than ten drivers. Your opportunities are not limited to working for trucking companies; many businesses also hire local drivers. The good news is that everyone is now eagerly looking for drivers. In fact, truck driving has among the largest number of job openings of any occupation.

At the start of the twenty-first century, more than eighty thousand new local and long-haul truck drivers were needed each year, and a severe shortage of drivers to replace those who were leaving the field existed. How long truck drivers will be in such demand will depend on the strength of the economy. In good times, when the economy is strong, more freight is moved by trucks, and companies tend to hire more drivers. If the economy slows, companies hire fewer drivers or even lay off drivers. Overall, the employment of truck drivers through the year 2008 should grow, as the amount of freight carried by trucks is expected to increase. The increased use of rail, air, and ship transportation also requires more local drivers to pick up and deliver these shipments. Because truckdriving does not require education beyond high school, you can expect to compete for those jobs that have the most attractive earnings and working conditions.

The one area in which the demand for truck drivers will grow slowly is in driver-sales worker jobs. This is because companies are increasingly splitting their responsibilities among other workers. Sales, ordering, and customer service tasks are being shifted to sales and office staffs, and regular truck drivers are being used to make deliveries to customers.

The Earnings Picture

Local truck driving jobs vary greatly in terms of earnings, weekly work hours, and the quality of equipment operated. As you gain experience in this career, you will become a more-valued worker and enjoy increased earnings. Also, the size and type of truck that you drive affects your pay, with those driving larger trucks earning more money. Employers pay local truck drivers an hourly rate and extra pay for working overtime, usually after forty hours. Benefits including health insurance and sick and vacation leave are common in the trucking industry. Plus, performance-related bonuses are given, especially for those with safe driving records. The average weekly earnings of truck drivers exceed $550 per week. Some drivers earn more than $1,500 per week. About 21 percent of all truckers are union members, with most belonging to the International Brotherhood of Teamsters.

A Career as a Local Truck Driver

Brent Lindke is an experienced local truck driver. This is an excellent career choice for him, as he has always loved to drive and doesn't want to be in an office all day. Besides, this career choice has allowed him to achieve his childhood dream of driving a big truck. Before taking his present job with a company that distributes wood products to building supply companies such as Home Depot, Brent worked in the industry as a long-haul driver. He firmly believes that he was hired for his current job because he had so much driving experience.

At the present time, Brent is driving a tractor-trailer that is so new that he hasn't had time yet to install his CB radio. The cab has two seats, but only his seat is an air-ride seat that takes much of the bounce out of driving on uneven roads. Although the panel appears to have a great number of gauges to study, the only additions beyond what a car might have are air gauges that tell him if he has sufficient air for breaking. As he drives along, Brent frequently checks the air, water, and oil gauges to make sure that he catches a potential problem before it can occur. He also watches the speedometer because drivers can lose their jobs and licenses if they have too many speeding tickets. There is an engine governor that will not let him go over sixty-eight miles per hour.

Brent always concentrates intently on what is happening on the road. While the drivers of passenger cars typically observe only several cars in front of them, he must observe at least a distance of two blocks because it takes him so much longer to stop. Brent, however, does not just look forward; he must also use the side mirrors to locate the cars beside and behind his truck. This is not totally successful because trucks have lots of blind spots where drivers simply cannot see cars no matter how many mirrors they have.

On the Job with Brent

The job of driving a tractor-trailer in one of the most congested traffic areas in Northern California is not an easy task. Also, being a local driver may involve more organization, paperwork, lifting, and long days than you ever imagined. Brent usually works four very long days of thirteen to fifteen hours each week; however, by law he can only drive for ten of those hours. In a typical day, he will make from ten to eighteen stops on a route that goes from Sacramento to as far south as San Jose and back to Sacramento. This usually involves driving from 300 to 360 miles, although it could be as many as 500 miles.

On workdays, Brent gets up at 2:15 A.M. so he can be at the terminal by 3:00 A.M. Although the truck is already loaded, he must make sure that the load is properly strapped down. He also has to check the truck from bumper to bumper to make sure that it is safe to be on the road. And he studies the papers detailing where he will stop, what will be delivered at each stop, and the location of the products on the truck. By 3:45 A.M., Brent is usually ready to pull out of the terminal to begin his route.

Driving to His First Delivery

When he is on the road in the congested Bay Area, Brent is more inclined to listen to the radio for traffic reports than to talk on the CB with other drivers. The start of his route is fairly easy because he drives on an Interstate highway and there is very little traffic so early in the morning. In fact, he is so early on the day described here that the usually crowded toll area of the San Francisco Bay Bridge is quite empty. By 6:30 A.M., the traffic will begin to pick up. Not only does Brent leave Sacramento early to avoid traffic, he also is supposed to be in and out of his first stop by 7:00 A.M., as tractor-trailers are not allowed on city streets where his first delivery will be made after that time.

The First Delivery

Brent drives through San Francisco on a freeway to arrive at his first stop at a twenty-four-hour Home Depot store at 5:45 A.M. As usual, there are many other trucks in front of him, and he will have to wait his turn. He immediately checks in and finds out where he should park. Most days, he will have to wait from forty-five minutes to one hour to get unloaded at this busy store. Brent uses this time to update his logbook, which is a record of what he is doing every fifteen minutes throughout the workday. He will also chat with other drivers and perhaps eat something for breakfast. During the waiting time, Brent continually inches the truck forward until it is time for it to be unloaded. Then, he puts on work gloves and pulls back the truck's side curtains so the forklift driver can easily remove a pallet of cedar closet liners. As soon as the driver signs the appropriate paperwork, Brent begins to maneuver away from the docking area. The entire delivery has taken forty-five minutes. To leave, he has to make a sharp left turn around the building and avoid hitting piles of products that are stacked along his path. Some backing up is required to make the turn.

The Second Delivery

Brent only has to travel across a parking lot to reach his second delivery site. Since so many trucks are ahead of his, he decides to unload the products himself in order to arrive early for his next delivery. This requires him to get a lumber cart and lift four heavy doors (seventy-five to one hundred pounds each) from the truck and place them on the cart. It takes him about ten minutes to unload the products and another ten minutes for the company to check that the product is not damaged and to complete the paperwork.

The Third Delivery

When Brent gets back on the road again, he backtracks to a building supply store in San Francisco that will not start unloading trucks until 8:00 A.M. Traffic is beginning to pick up on the San Francisco freeway, and rain is now falling, making driving more challenging. Because Brent's truck cannot enter the store's loading area, it will have to be unloaded on a narrow one-block street. He has already considered which direction he must go on the street in order for the load to be easily accessible to the fork-lift driver. Once again, there are trucks in line ahead of him. Also, the congestion on the street is unbelievable, with trucks parked on both sides and cars weaving between them. Brent has to direct a fellow trucker who is backing a flatbed down an adjacent alley in order to find a space to park his truck for unloading. He just avoids having to parallel park in a narrow space, which is one of the most difficult things for truckers to do.

After a wait of about twenty minutes, a forklift operator unloads three pallets of building materials. Because a prior shipment was incorrect, time must also be spent loading it on the truck to be returned to the home terminal. It is Brent's responsibility to make sure it is strapped securely in the truck.

The Remainder of the Day

Throughout the day, while Brent waits for his truck to be unloaded, he will continually update his log, study the paperwork for the remaining deliveries, and eat the food he has brought with him.

Brent's workday began at 3:00 A.M. By 8:15, he had made three deliveries. He will need to make ten more before he can return home. He will face heavy traffic until about 10:00 A.M. Then it will be lighter, except for the noon hour and commuter rush periods. Brent will probably not be back at the supply terminal until about 6:30 P.M., and he will have spent more than fifteen hours on the job during this typical day.

Career Advice

Brent admits that being a local truck driver is not the right career for everyone. Although he loves being a road warrior and being able to be home each evening, the major downside of this job for him is having to get up so early four days a week. He advises anyone considering a career in this field to find a local driver and ride with him or her for a day or more to see exactly what this career is like. And if you are still in school, he believes that you should pay close attention to mathematics, physics, and geography, as you will use these subjects every day as a truck driver.

Another Route to Being a Local Truck Driver

Brent Lindke learned how to drive trucks by going to a driving school. This is not the route that Kurt Zimmerman followed in first becoming a local driver and then a long-haul driver. He learned to drive on the job. After completing high school and some college, Kurt worked in sales. One day, he saw a line outside the trucking firm next door to his office. Because he was curious, he discovered that the company was looking for workers and offering a very good wage. Kurt decided to interview and was hired on the spot for a job as a fueler at a trucking terminal. Company personnel informally taught Kurt, and soon he was driving trucks to and from the fueling station. He admits that he ground a lot of gears while learning to drive. Kurt also discovered that he really liked the idea of becoming a driver and obtained a license. Because he displayed initiative, the trucking company put him on the road with the safety director, and he learned by trial and error to drive a truck with a forty-eight-foot trailer.

Kurt Becomes a Local Truck Driver

One day while Kurt was working as a fueler, the trucking company had a load that needed to be driven immediately to Rockford, Illinois, from the Chicago area where he worked. The dispatcher asked Kurt to handle this assignment even though Kurt explained that he was not a very experienced driver and had never been to Rockford. The dispatcher said this was the way for him to learn, so Kurt soon found himself on the road following a map and making his first delivery. The entire round trip was a hundred miles.

Because Kurt completed this first trip successfully, the company soon asked him to become a driver doing local jobs within one hundred miles miles of the terminal. He delivered all kinds of products to homes, hospitals, and businesses. Besides driving, Kurt had to help load and unload the cargo, which required a strong back. Occasionally, he needed a helper because the loads were so heavy. He especially remembers having to lift cases of books up several flights of stairs. His job also involved doing a lot of map reading to find delivery places. Often, he would need to contact the local police to find out what route he should take because trucks are prohibited on many city streets. Sometimes, he would even need to obtain a permit to drive on side streets.

For more than thirteen years, Kurt was a local truck driver. During this time, he had several memorable experiences, as all drivers do. One time, he was delivering more than fifty thousand baby chickens to a research facility. Unfortunately, several of the boxes came open, and six hundred chickens were suddenly loose in the truck. It was not easy for him to get so many chickens back in their boxes. Kurt also remembers opening the door of a truck he was unloading and coming face-to-face with a rattlesnake that had hitched a ride from Texas. During his years as a local trucker, Kurt especially enjoyed having such close contact with the people receiving the products that he delivered. He left this position to become a long-haul driver because, as a true road warrior, he wanted to see more places.

A Career Driving a Produce Truck

Don Benson is a local truck driver who delivers produce for the Piazza Produce Company of Indianapolis. He drives an eighteen-foot, low-profile truck with a refrigerated box. His route will take him to several cities and small towns in Northeast Indiana. Don's day begins at 4:00 A.M., when he gets to the produce company where he performs a pretrip check of his truck, including lights, tires, and flashers. The produce has already been loaded into the truck by the overnight crew. Once Don has picked up the invoices for the day's deliveries, it is time for this road warrior to begin his route.

At each delivery point, Don must unload the produce listed on that customer's invoice. Using a two-wheeled hand truck, he takes the order into schools, restaurants, and businesses. At some stops, he must rotate the stock on the shelves. At others, he only has to place the produce in the designated receiving area so that the employees can then store it properly. When his route is complete, Don returns to the terminal and does a post-trip check of the truck. If there are any mechanical problems, he must fill out a form requesting repairs.

Don's route requires him to travel about 315 miles every day. Accidents and bad weather can really slow him down, keeping him on the road as late as 7:00 P.M. and forcing him to work a fifteen-hour day. As Don travels along his route on interstate highways and city streets, he is very aware of the other drivers on the road who don't want to get stuck behind his truck. It is not unusual for him to be cut off by drivers who are in a hurry and make risky maneuvers. These drivers frustrate Don because he feels like he must second-guess them in order to avoid accidents. He also has to be very cautious in the heavy traffic he often encounters on narrow city streets.

An Unfortunate Accident

Don's most memorable experience as a produce driver was wrecking his truck. While he was trying to avoid an accident with a vehicle coming onto a snowy, slippery interstate, Don lost control of the truck, spun across the road, and hit a semitractor-trailer. His much smaller truck was totally destroyed; fortunately, he only received minor injuries. Although the accident was very serious, Don was back behind the wheel of a produce truck four days later.

Career Pluses

Don learned about his job from his brother, who worked for the company. He knew that he would like this job because he would get to be outside throughout the day. Now that he is on the job, Don really likes driving his truck, seeing the scenery along the route, and meeting lots of people along the way. This road warrior feels a great sense of freedom and relaxation as he drives his route and delivers produce. Don also likes being fully responsible for making his deliveries as quickly and efficiently as possible. In this job, he is his own boss when he is out on his route.

Driving for a Local Company

Most of the drivers that have been described in this chapter work for trucking companies. There are also many job opportunities to drive for other companies picking up and delivering goods. Some of these jobs will require you to drive a tractor-trailer, while others involve driving smaller trucks, vans, and pickups. Here is a list of the types of companies where you might find a job as a local truck driver.

milk companies	hardware stores
furniture stores	gasoline companies
cleaners	flower shops
department stores	local movers
lumberyards	nurseries
waste removal companies	construction companies
building supply companies	tire companies

grocery suppliers

office supply companies

appliance stores

plumbing companies

beverage companies

commercial bakeries

For More Information

You can find out more about job opportunities for local truck drivers from local trucking companies and local offices of the state employment service.

More information on career opportunities in truck driving may be obtained from:

American Trucking Associations, Inc.
2200 Mill Road
Alexandria, VA 22314
www.truckline.com

American Trucking Association Foundation
600 Roosevelt Avenue
Pawtucket, RI 02860

The Professional Truck Driver Institute, a nonprofit organization established by the trucking industry, manufacturers, and others, certifies truck driver training programs meeting industry standards. A free list of certified tractor-trailer driver training programs and a booklet, *Careers in Trucking*, may be obtained from:

Professional Truck Driver Institute
2200 Mill Road
Alexandria, VA 22314
www.ptdi.org

CHAPTER FOUR

Careers for Long-Haul Truck Drivers

L ocal truck drivers work close to home. Long-haul truckers crisscross the United States bringing all kinds of goods from one area of the country to another. They even carry products to Mexico and Canada. If you buy furniture in North Carolina, it will be a long-haul truck driver who transports it to your home in New Mexico. If you eat an orange in Minneapolis, it was probably brought there from Florida, California, or Texas by a long-haul trucker. These drivers also transport new cars from Detroit to Iowa, seafood from the Gulf to New York City, and computers from Silicon Valley to Atlanta. They bring products from manufacturers to retailers and raw materials to processing plants. Whenever you are on a highway or freeway, you will see long-haul truck drivers doing the business of keeping the goods in this country moving. Before the development of the interstate highway system in the mid-1950s, most goods were moved across the country by rail. This is no longer true. Trucks have now totally eclipsed the railroads as cross-country carriers of most goods. Being a long-haul truck driver will not only keep you on the move, it will also help keep commerce in America moving.

Trucking Companies

There are nearly fifty thousand long-distance trucking companies. As a long-haul driver on the move, you can work for a company that delivers freight across the country, a regional firm that will make deliveries in several states, or a company that concentrates on delivering goods within a single state. The companies range in size from giants like Schneider National Carriers and Yellow Freight Systems with thousands of drivers to small companies with only one or two drivers. You will also have the opportunity to choose between working for a company that hauls its own products and one that carries goods for many different shippers.

Long-distance trucking companies transport a wide variety of goods in numerous types of equipment from refrigerated trailers to flatbeds. These companies operate as both truckload (TL) or less than truckload (LTL) carriers. The truckload carriers move large amounts of goods directly to their destinations, usually with no stops in between. They carry full single loads that are not combined with other shipments. Less than truckload carriers pick up multiple shipments and take them to a terminal, where they are unloaded and then reloaded by destination. Then the shipments are carried to distant terminals near their destinations. Local truck drivers complete the delivery chain.

The trucking company where you choose to work may also offer a wide variety of services designed to improve the efficient transfer of goods. For example, with "just-in-time" shipping, trucking companies deliver goods from suppliers just in time for their use. For a driver, this creates the responsibility of meeting tight schedules without fail.

The Lifestyle of Long-Haul Truck Drivers

Long-haul truck driving is no longer a solitary job for all drivers. More and more companies are using two drivers on very long runs—one drives while the other sleeps in a berth behind the cab. "Sleeper" runs may last for days or even weeks, usually with the truck stopping only for fuel, food, loading, and unloading.

While some long-distance drivers have regular runs transporting freight to the same city, others perform unscheduled runs and may have no idea of where they will go on a run. For example, a driver may set out from Chicago carrying books to Ohio. From there, the dispatcher may send the driver to Miami with tires. Before a run ends, the driver may also go to Dallas, Phoenix, cross into Mexico, then on to Los Angeles, Seattle, and Omaha before returning to Chicago.

The Tasks of Long-Haul Truck Drivers

Long-haul drivers can expect to spend most of their working hours behind the wheel; however, they may load or unload their cargo after arriving at a destination. This is especially true if you decide to haul specialty cargo because you are likely to be the only one at the destination familiar with the procedure or certified to handle it. As an auto-transport driver, for example, you would be expected to drive and position cars on the trailers and head ramps and remove them at the dealerships.

The Professional Truck Driver Institute lists the following duties as the primary functions of long-haul truck drivers:

1. Read and interpret control systems

2. Perform vehicle inspections

3. Exercise basic control

4. Execute shifting

5. Back and dock tractor trailer

6. Couple trailer

7. Uncouple trailer

8. Perform visual search

9. Manage and adjust vehicle speed

10. Manage and adjust vehicle space relations

11. Check and maintain vehicle systems and components

12. Diagnose and report malfunctions

13. Identify potential driving hazards and perform emergency maneuvers

14. Identify and adjust to difficult and extreme driving conditions

15. Handle and document cargo

16. Act responsibly with accident scenes and reporting procedures

17. Be aware of and responsible for environmental issues

18. Plan trips and make appropriate decisions

19. Use effective communication and public relations skills

20. Manage personal resources and cope with life on the road

21. Record and maintain hours of service requirement

Work Conditions for Long-Haul Drivers

As a long-haul driver, expect to frequently travel at night, on holidays, and on weekends to avoid traffic delays and to deliver cargo on time. How long you drive each day and week is regulated by the U.S. Department of Commerce. In general, you will be not able to work more than sixty hours in any seven-day period and will be required to rest eight hours for every ten hours of driving. If you are like most drivers on long runs, you will work close to the maximum time permitted because what you earn is typically based on the number of miles or hours you drive.

On the road, long-haul drivers must cope with variable weather and traffic conditions. For example, all in one day, they may experience driving in an unusual spring snowstorm in the mountains and on crowded city streets. Boredom, loneliness, and fatigue are part of this career. Also, an adjustment must be made to spending so little time at home. Some self-employed long-haul truck drivers who own and operate their trucks spend most of the year away from home. Nevertheless, most drivers enjoy the independence and lack of supervision found in long-distance driving.

Design improvements in newer trucks and technological advances are doing much to reduce the stress of long-distance driving. Many of the newer trucks are virtual miniapartments on wheels, equipped with refrigerators, televisions, and bunks. Satellites and Global Positioning Systems (GPS) link many of these state-of-the-art vehicles with company headquarters. Today, troubleshooting, directions, weather reports, and other important communications can be delivered to trucks anywhere they are located within seconds. Furthermore, drivers can easily communicate with dispatchers to discuss delivery schedules and courses of action in the event of mechanical problems. The satellite linkup also allows dispatchers to track a truck's location, fuel consumption, and engine performance.

Job Qualifications

Qualifications for a job as a long-haul truck driver are far more demanding than those for local drivers. You must meet the following minimum requirements prescribed in the Federal Motor Carrier Safety Regulations.

- *Age:* Drivers must be at least twenty-one years of age to drive trucks across state lines.

- *License:* All drivers must obtain a commercial driver's license (CDL) issued by the state in which they live. To qualify for a CDL, you will have to pass a written test on rules and regulations, and then demonstrate that you can operate a commercial truck safely. Contact your state Department of Motor Vehicles for more information about this license.

- *Physical Requirements*: Drivers will need to pass a physical examination once every two years. The main physical requirements include good hearing, 20/40 vision with or without corrective lenses, and a seventy-degree field of vision in each eye. Drivers cannot be color-blind and must be able to hear a forced whisper in one ear at not less than five feet with or without a hearing aid. Drivers must have normal use of arms and legs and normal blood pressure. You will not be able to be an interstate truck driver if you have epilepsy or diabetes controlled by insulin.

- *Driving Record*: Drivers may not have been convicted of a felony involving the use of a motor vehicle; driving under the influence of drugs or alcohol; or hit-and-run driving that resulted in injury or death.

- *Education*: All drivers must be able to read and speak English well enough to read road signs, prepare reports, and communicate with law enforcement officers and the public.

- *Safety*: Drivers must learn and comply with the safety rules of the U.S. Department of Transportation and take a written examination on the department's Motor Carrier Safety Regulations.

- *Substance Abuse*: Federal regulations require employers to test their drivers for alcohol and drug use as a condition of employment and require periodic random tests while on duty. Drivers must not have been convicted of a crime using drugs.

For more information on the qualifications of drivers, see Part 391 of the Federal Motor Carrier Safety Regulations. Also, you will find that many trucking companies have even higher standards than those listed in this book. Many firms require drivers to be at least twenty-five years old, be able to lift heavy objects, and have driven trucks for three to five years. Plus, companies often prefer to hire high school graduates and may require annual physical examinations.

Training

Very few jobs entail so much personal responsibility as being the driver of a long-distance truck. While drivers can now get advice more easily from dispatchers, customers, other truck drivers, and highway patrol officers, in the end, it is the drivers who have their hands on the wheels. They have the difficult task of bringing a more than $100,000 vehicle with all its cargo to a receiver on time, undamaged, and safely. This requires training.

In some states, prospective drivers are required to complete a training course in basic truckdriving before being issued a CDL. In Maine, for example, license applicants must complete an eight-week course certified by the Professional Truck Driver Institute. These courses provide training that meets Federal Highway Administration guidelines for training tractor-trailer drivers. You can find a list of schools offering these courses in Appendix B. You should also look at the checklist for finding quality tractor-trailer driver training school courses in Appendix A as not all courses meet these standards.

Attending a training school is not the only way to learn how to become a long-haul truck driver. Some drivers have been trained in the military. Large trucking companies also may have their own formal training programs that prospective drivers attend. Other companies assign experienced drivers to teach and mentor newer drivers.

Going into Business for Yourself

While the overwhelming majority of all long-distance drivers will elect to work for a trucking company or a firm hauling its own products, some purchase a truck and go into business for themselves. Although many of these owner-operators are successful, some fail to cover expenses and eventually go out of business. To succeed as an owner-operator, you will need to have a good business sense as well as truck driving experience. Taking courses in accounting, business, and business mathematics is helpful. Plus, knowledge of truck mechanics can help owner-operators save money by being able to perform their own routine maintenance and minor repairs.

Job Outlook

In recent years, long-distance trucking companies have experienced considerable difficulty in recruiting adequately skilled drivers. Although truck driving pays relatively well, many people leave the career because of the lengthy periods away from home, long hours of driving, and the negative public image drivers face. While opportunities for long-haul drivers will continue to grow about as fast as the average for all occupations through the year 2008, there are two cautions: 1) Growth could slow in this area if rail cars increasingly ship loaded trailers across the country. 2) A downturn in the economy would result in fewer drivers being hired. Independent owner-operators are particularly vulnerable to economic slowdowns.

The Earnings Picture

Long-haul truck drivers typically earn more than local drivers. Most are paid by the mile. The rate per mile can vary greatly from employer to employer and may even increase with the type of cargo.

Typically, earnings increase with mileage driven, seniority, and the size and type of truck driven. Those drivers with the most seniority earn the most because they get the best assignments. A senior driver working for a unionized freight company might be able to earn as much as $60,000 to $70,000 a year. A few drivers work on commission. These drivers earn a fixed percentage of the profits their employers make on each trip.

A Career as a Long-Haul Driver

Kurt Zimmerman's career as a local truck driver was described in Chapter 3. While he was driving locally, another company recruited him to become an auto-transport driver hauling cars from a port in Maryland to the Chicago area. The auto carrier, itself, was not like the auto carriers you usually see on the road; instead, ten cars were hung inside on pegs. Kurt and his codriver did not put the cars in the carrier; that was done robotically. Speed was of the essence in this job, as it is in all long-distance hauls. The two drivers would leave the Chicago area on Sunday afternoon and travel the thousand miles to Maryland, only stopping for fuel and quick meals. After the carrier was loaded with cars, they would begin their return trip. Kurt might have a few hours at home on Wednesday before he began another trip. His only time off was Saturday and part of Sunday. After a little more than two years of being on the road most of the time, Kurt decided to take a job working in a truck yard fueling and preparing vehicles for the road so he could have more time at home. He also did some local truck driving.

A New Driving Job

The lure of the open road drew Kurt back into long-distance driving. It was not difficult for him to get a job. With his experience, he soon had eight job offers. This is not unusual for a good driver with an excellent safety record. Kurt chose to work for a regional carrier owned by a family. Even though the owners had eight thousand employees, they knew their drivers. Kurt had such good rapport with them that he could call on the phone and they knew who he was. Another advantage to this job of driving double trailers from Chicago to Detroit or Cleveland was that he could be home every night or every other night. Also, he didn't have to load or unload freight, as he was driving between truck terminals. If he had to stay overnight, he would go to a hotel, sleep eight hours, and then be back on the road again. Unfortunately, this family-owned firm of one hundred years went out of business after Kurt had worked for them for more than two years. Once again, he was looking for a job.

A Job with a Very Large Trucking Company

Yellow Freight Systems is the world's largest carrier of less-than-truckload shipments. The company has about six hundred terminals. Local drivers bring shipments to company terminals where they are loaded onto trucks for the long-haul drivers to take to their destinations. Kurt became one of the approximately 150 driver teams working out of Chicago. He began driving from six thousand to seven thousand miles a week with a codriver. On these long trips, Kurt might leave from Chicago and go out West to Seattle, Portland, Tucson, and back home.

Working with a codriver can be challenging. The company tries to match personalities and to consider smoking preferences when they put driving teams together. The drivers can also choose codrivers for three-month periods. Kurt points out that it is very important for drivers to get along, or they may have a week or more of misery. He believes that you need to have a very accepting personality to handle being so close to another person twenty-four hours a day. You may find yourself with a nonstop talker or a quiet individual. And some drivers are extremely neat, while others may be messy.

On the Road with a Codriver

When two drivers start out on a long trip, the freshest driver begins the trip and will usually drive ten hours. When it is Kurt's rest time, he tries to sleep for eight hours but finds it difficult on a bouncing bed. For the remainder of the time, he watches video tapes of TV programs that he has missed, does crossword puzzles, and listens to books on tape. The drivers usually change positions at a truck stop after a shower, meal, and refueling. Kurt believes that there is truth to the statement that motorists should stop at restaurants where they see a lot of trucks parked. Both he and his fellow drivers spend considerable time in discovering the very best places to eat along highways.

Drivers Are Responsible Road Warriors

Drivers are always very concerned with road safety. At each stop, Kurt and his codriver will walk around the tractor trailer carefully to check that there are no problems. They will also clean the taillights so other drivers can see them. Kurt tries to begin each trip well rested. If he becomes sleepy, he will exercise, drink coffee, or take a quick nap. He definitely knows when it is not safe for him to drive. Besides responsible driving, Kurt's company supports the efforts of their drivers to help motorists in trouble if they can safely pull off the road. Once or twice a week, he will help someone change a tire. Unfortunately, when he is driving at night, he usually needs to call the highway patrol at least once to report drivers who are weaving across lanes or driving in an erratic manner, indicating that they are probably drunk.

A Look at Several Trips

In order to spend more time at home with his family, which now includes five adopted children, Kurt started driving shorter routes from his home terminal in the Chicago area. He drives these routes alone in a day cab. Rather than have a definite route, he is on call twenty-four hours a day, seven days a week.

Chicago to Buffalo and back: This trip pulling three trailers started at 2:00 P.M. on Sunday and ended twelve hours later. Kurt drove through Canada, as this route has less traffic and is shorter, even though one-half hour to an hour must be spent going through customs. The trip was slowed down by an unexpected snowstorm that lasted two hours and by stopping briefly to help a motorist change a tire. After arriving at the terminal, Kurt took a shuttle bus to the hotel, where he swam, worked out, and slept to meet the eight-hour rest requirement before going back out on the road. Then, with two hours' notice, Kurt returned to Chicago, arriving home at 11:00 P.M. on Monday.

Chicago to Cleveland and back: After resting at home for eight hours, Kurt's next trip was to Cleveland and back. On this trip, as on all trips, he can only drive ten hours before resting eight.

Omaha, St. Paul, Eau Claire, Green Bay, and back: Before starting this trip that took him to Nebraska, through Minnesota, and on to Wisconsin, Kurt was home for twelve hours. He spent one night on the road and then took two days off before starting another trip.

Why this Road Warrior Loves His Job

If you want to find out what the United States and Canada are really like, being a long-haul truck driver makes it a reality. Kurt speaks with awe of the wonders he has seen over the years. He knows what it's like when the sun rises over the Grand Canyon. He has observed thirty-feet snowfalls in the Canadian Rockies and deer and elk on Donner Pass in the Sierras. Kurt considers dispatchers as his travel agents and says that he is being paid to be a tourist. He has taken so many pictures over the years of what he has seen that his CB handle is "Flash."

Beginning a Driving Career as a Long-Haul Truck Driver

While Kurt began his career as a local truck driver, Brent Lindke (also discussed in Chapter 3) started his as a long-haul driver. Brent's first job after high school was driving an ambulance. To handle this job, he needed to become an emergency medical technician and to obtain an ambulance driver's license. His first job set the pattern for future jobs, as Brent knew that he loved driving and did not want to work in an office. He has also worked as the driver of a fire truck for a volunteer fire department.

After making the decision that he wanted to become a truck driver, Brent enrolled in a truck driving school. He believes that this was the correct decision as the school gave him sufficient time behind the wheel to master the intricacies of driving a tractor-trailer. Before Brent even completed the school, he had three job offers, which shows how great the demand is for drivers. He accepted the offer of a Salt Lake City company, where he received even more training. Brent began riding with a trainer who helped him learn how to load a truck properly, to do the necessary company paperwork, and to handle logbooks and billing. Time was also devoted to learning how to plan trips. Quite often, there is more than one route to a destination, so he had to learn how to find the fastest one. After just two and a half weeks with the trainer, Brent was sent out on the road driving alone from coast to coast. Most drivers spent six weeks with a trainer; however, his prior driving experiences accelerated Brent's training time.

For Brent, driving long-distance routes was lonely. He would be out from three to six weeks at a time and then would only be home for two or three days. Brent switched to another trucking company that promised he would be home every two weeks. While working at this company, he saw that local truck drivers had jobs that more closely matched his personal needs to have more time at home. Subsequently, Brent became a local truck driver.

A Husband and Wife Team Hauling Livestock

Roger Pitman is a long-haul truck driver; however, he doesn't drive alone. Instead, right by his side and sharing in some of the driving is his wife, Martha. Both have literally spent their lives around trucks. In fact, Roger was driving a truck in the hay field of the family farm so workers could load bales of hay on it when he was only eight. By the time he was sixteen, his father was raising tomatoes and Roger was driving loads of tomatoes to canneries. Martha's first experience with trucks was being taught to drive her brother's lumber truck. Then, she gained additional truck driving experience by hauling wheat, corn, and soybeans to elevators.

After high school, Martha and Roger married, and he began to work on his father's dairy farm. Part of this job involved hauling farm products and driving his family's trailer truck to pick up and deliver agricultural products like fertilizer to neighboring farmers. After deciding to quit farming, Roger worked as a forester and then sold livestock feed before deciding that what he really wanted was a career as a truck driver.

Roger's First Driving Jobs

Roger went to work for a small trucking company with eight to ten trucks hauling grain from Indiana elevators to Chicago or Cincinnati. He was considered a local truck driver because he stayed within two hundred to three hundred miles of his home base in Indianapolis and returned home after each run. It was his responsibility to oversee the loading and unloading of the grain. Once he arrived in Chicago or Cincinnati, he would sleep while he sat in line up to half a day at the big grain elevators waiting to unload. Then, he would hurry back to Indiana to get another load. Hauling grain is dusty and dirty work, and it is also seasonal. When he was not hauling grain, Roger drove a flatbed truck with a sleeper cab hauling a variety of products, including steel, and a car van hauling auto parts. At this time, Martha's association with trucking was limited to working as a cashier at a truck stop.

A friend convinced Roger to change jobs, and they began working as a team hauling produce across the country for a trucking company. They would pick up melons, plums, and other produce in California and take it to cities on the East Coast, where a dispatcher would find a load for them to haul back to the West Coast. The round-trip would take seven days. They were not being paid for the hours they drove but on commission. At first, this job was quite profitable; however, after a while they were not making enough money, as layovers on the West Coast became too lengthy because of the weather and difficulty in finding loads to haul. Roger quit this job and began a search immediately for another driving job.

Roger stopped driving produce on Friday. On Saturday, he talked to a livestock hauling company that indicated there might be work for him the following week. On Tuesday, the company called and asked him to report with boots, coveralls, and gloves to start out with an experienced driver on a short haul. Getting a new job so quickly is not unusual, as there is such a strong demand for experienced truck drivers.

Driving Livestock East of the Mississippi

Driving livestock is more than a driving job. First of all, Roger goes to a buying station that has bought sheep, pigs, or cows to sell to meat packers. Although farmers have brought the animals to this station, it is the driver's responsibility to load the animals aboard the trailer for the trip to the packer. The trailer has three decks for sheep and pigs; however, when cows are being hauled, the driver has to convert the trailer to two decks. Besides loading the animals on the trailer—a job requiring him to wear boots, gloves, and overalls—he also unloads them at the packers.

All of his farm experience has been helpful in this aspect of the job. When Roger first began hauling livestock, he would only haul animals one way. In recent years, he has begun to haul feeder cattle from Virginia and West Virginia back to Indiana and Illinois to be fattened. In this way, he is able to have loads both ways from 70 to 75 percent of the time. And he will only drive an empty rig for one hundred to three hundred miles after unloading the animals he has brought from the Midwest.

Roger works on commission. He receives a predetermined percentage of the profit the trucking company makes on each load he hauls. To him, working on commission is a real incentive to produce. The more loads he hauls, the more money he makes.

Working as a Husband and Wife Driving Team

When Roger first began hauling livestock, he worked with another driver. Then, for a number of years, he worked alone. After their children completed school, Martha left her job at the truck stop, worked for a brief time at a store, and then began going with Roger on trips. At first, she just rode with him. Then she obtained her commercial driver's license, and Roger began to teach her how to drive the truck on straight roads. Although he does most of the driving, Martha now drives on low-risk interstates where there is less traffic and on better weather days. Her other responsibility is to keep records of the number of miles that they drive in each state. This is the information that the individual states use to levy taxes on trucks. As far as their other responsibilities go, Roger keeps the driver's log and loads and unloads the livestock. Martha does not work directly with the animals because it can be dangerous work.

On the road, Roger and Martha live in their truck, which has a very comfortable sleeping area that is carpeted and air-conditioned and has a television set. They do not have a refrigerator or microwave to use in the preparation of meals because the vibration from the road severely limits the life span of these appliances. Instead, they have discovered the best places to eat along the routes they take going from the Midwest to the East Coast and back.

Roger and Martha never know what their next driving assignment will be until a dispatcher calls. They also work both weekdays and weekends. On most of their trips, they travel between three thousand and thirty-five hundred miles; however, trips can be shorter. In an average month, they will work from twenty-three to twenty-five days. Their workweeks and hours on the job each day are definitely longer than for most workers.

A Way of Life

Being on the move is a way of life for Roger and Martha. As Martha explains, "Once driving is in your blood, you can't get it out." Roger especially likes the independence of being their own bosses on the road. Martha likes seeing the ever-changing countryside. While most of their trips are routine, they have experienced several memorable moments. Once they were going to Rockville, Indiana, to pick up a load of pigs. Before they arrived, a tornado had gone through the town and knocked out the electric power. They then had the difficult task of loading the pigs in the middle of the night with only their flashlights for light. Roger and Martha are true road warriors.

Combining Driving and Another Career

For ten months of the year, Roger Harrington has two careers. He is both a long-haul driver and a mechanic on a drag-racing team. As a driver of one of the team's two eighteen-wheelers, he transports racing cars, car parts, tires, tools, oil, fuel, uniforms, and everything else it takes to operate on the road. During racing season, he will be gone from the team's headquarters in Indianapolis for one to six weeks, depending on the racing schedule. When the team leaves Indianapolis for a race, each truck has two drivers so they can drive straight through to the racetrack.

Once the team arrives at the track, Roger works as one of the eight mechanics programming the cars for the race. Then during the race, he and the other mechanics act as the pit crew. Typically, the qualifying runs are held on Friday and Saturday and the four runs to the finals on Sunday. After each race, the team will return to Indianapolis the next day unless another race is scheduled for the following weekend. In that case, they will usually go on to the next racetrack.

Roger worked on the team as a mechanic before he became one of its drivers. When the team needed another long-haul driver, he obtained a learner's permit and was taught how to drive by one of the team's experienced drivers. Not only did Roger see learning to drive a truck as a way to help the team, he also believed that it might lead to other career opportunities. His two careers have let him travel around the country and enjoy the tremendous exhilaration of seeing a car that he has worked on do well.

Two Industry-Acclaimed Drivers

America's Road Team is a select group of outstanding professional truck drivers who have been nominated by the American Trucking Associations (ATA), the national trade association of the trucking industry, to spread the word about highway safety and improve the image of the trucking industry. As members of this team, Marty and Lisa Fortun often speak to students on high school career days. Besides explaining what it is like to be a truck driver, they point out the importance of studying math, foreign language, and geography in preparation for this career. They tell the students how they use math in determining when and where they will stop for fuel and how the load should be distributed correctly. They explain how helpful studying a foreign language is in order to be prepared to drive in Mexico and Quebec. And they spell out how helpful it is to know geography in order to anticipate what the terrain will be like along the trip route.

Because their safety records are so outstanding, both have received many industry awards for safety and their skills. Marty has driven 2.4 million without an accident, and Lisa has driven 1.4 million miles without an accident.

Trucking Is a Family Tradition

Marty's dad, younger brother, and many aunts and uncles are all truck drivers. In fact, his first job as a long-haul driver was on a team with his father. Lisa's parents were a driving team just like she and Marty are today. Together, they drive a dedicated route, which involves following the same schedule each week. Every Sunday, they pull out of Green Bay, Wisconsin, pulling two trailers full of truck parts for two company terminals. They leave one in Seville, Ohio, and the other in Carlisle, Pennsylvania. At each terminal, they pick up a trailer already loaded with truck parts that can be repaired and return to Green Bay on Monday. They only stay in Green Bay long enough to pick up trailers to drive to Indianapolis, Indiana, and Charlotte, North Carolina, before returning to Green Bay on Wednesday.

Except for a six- to seven-hour layover that allows them to go home on Wednesday, they drive around the clock. Their final trip of the week is to Gary, Indiana, and West Memphis, Arkansas, which allows them to return to Green Bay very early Friday morning. They will then start this route all over again on Sunday morning. In recent years, the possibility of driving dedicated routes has increased, allowing drivers like Marty and Lisa to have more time at home. Because they love being on the move together, they think team driving is a great career.

Getting a Driving Job

Gus Staples got his start in the trucking business by learning how to operate and move heavy equipment during the Gulf War. When he returned home, he took his first trucking job delivering local freight in his hometown of Macon, Georgia. Gus found his present job by calling a phone number on the back of a truck he saw traveling through town. Two weeks after calling the number, he was driving his own tractor-trailer to Des Moines, Iowa, to deliver parts to a paper mill. Gus's story exemplifies the tremendous demand that exists for truck drivers and the many innovative ways trucking companies use to find drivers. On the job, Gus always drives the same tractor, but he changes trailers all the time. He prefers flatbed trailers because the loads are usually less weather sensitive and have less wind resistance traveling down the road.

For More Information

Begin by checking out the resources listed at the end of Chapter 3. These organizations can give you more information on career opportunities in trucking. To learn what the life of a long-haul truck driver is really like, it is very helpful to talk to someone who is actually engaged in this occupation.

Trucking companies vary in size from those with thousands of vehicles to those with only one truck. To learn more about what employment opportunities actually exist, visit the websites of several trucking companies as well as several on-line employment sites. Appendix C provides a list of the names and addresses of the top fifty truck carriers by revenue.

CHAPTER FIVE

Careers for Bus Drivers

B us drivers provide an important service. Millions of Americans depend on them every day to get safely to their jobs, schools, and other destinations. In fact, buses transport far more people than airlines or railroads. Buses are also the safest way to travel on streets, roads, and highways because they are involved in far fewer accidents than passenger cars, trucks, and motorcycles.

Imagine sitting behind the wheel of a forty-five-foot bus traveling down a narrow street in heavy, rush-hour traffic toward the next stop. There are twenty-five or thirty passengers behind you talking loudly, and someone is asking you where the next stop is. It is beginning to rain, and a car has just turned in front of the bus. Can you handle this demanding situation? If so, then driving a bus may be a good career choice for you.

If you elect to become a bus driver, four basic jobs are available. You can become a school bus driver transporting students to and from school and school-related activities; a local transit bus driver carrying people within a city; an intercity bus driver transporting people from city to city within a state or across the country; or a motorcoach driver taking passengers on tours or charter excursions. No matter which job you choose, you will be on the move behind the wheel almost every minute of your workday, whether you are driving a small ten-passenger vehicle, a very long city bus with trailer, or a forty-five-foot luxury motorcoach.

Types of Buses

The first bus was probably a stagecoach driven by a steam engine in about 1830. Of course, it had no resemblance to a modern bus. Nor did the early buses in the United States that were really cars lengthened to hold more passengers. By the 1920s, buses were mounted on a truck chassis, as modern school buses still are. Today, there are several types of buses. School buses carry fifty children and have special lights and safety features. Local transit buses have a low-ride platform, two entrances, low-back seats, and no space for luggage. Intercity and motor coach buses have high-back seats, luggage compartments and racks, reading lights, a rest room, and only one entrance. They typically carry about forty-seven passengers.

The Job of Driving a Bus

Bus drivers have a challenging task in coping with passengers and traffic. This job can be stressful and fatiguing. On the positive side, many drivers like working independently, knowing that everything happening on the bus is their responsibility. They are the captains, and the buses are their ships.

Passenger safety must be the primary concern of all bus drivers. They must drive defensively to prevent accidents in all kinds of traffic and weather. For the comfort and safety of their passengers, they have to avoid sudden stops or quick turns that could jar anyone on the bus. The other duties of bus drivers depend on where they work and whether their passengers are schoolchildren, commuters, intercity travelers, or tourists.

As a bus driver, your hours will depend upon your particular job. Some drivers have part-time jobs working less than twenty hours per week, while others have a regular full-time work schedule from week to week. A bus driver may also be on call-in status and have to work on short notice. Shift work and driving on weekends is common except for school bus drivers. With experience and seniority, drivers may be able to choose the routes they drive.

Job Qualifications

In order to become a bus driver, you must meet qualifications and standards set by state and federal regulations. If you operate a bus made to transport sixteen or more passengers, federal regulations require you to hold a commercial driver's license (CDL) from the state where you live. To qualify for a CDL, you will need to pass a written test on rules and regulations and then demonstrate that you can operate a bus safely. In order to prepare for the CDL, you will need to complete some behind-the-wheel training. A driver with a CDL must accompany trainees until they get this license.

Many states require a driver to be at least eighteen years old to drive within the state. Bus drivers who travel between states have to meet Federal Motor Carrier Safety Regulations, which require a driver to be at least twenty-one years old and pass a physical examination every two years. These regulations are described in detail in Chapter 4. Some states have guidelines that exceed federal regulations that the driver must comply with in order to be licensed within that state.

Beyond meeting licensing requirements, bus drivers need to have certain personal characteristics in order to handle this job. They need an even temperament and emotional stability because driving in heavy, fast-moving, or stop-and-go traffic and dealing with passengers from schoolchildren to senior citizens can be stressful. Drivers also need to have solid communication skills and know how to manage large groups of people.

Job Opportunities for Bus Drivers

More and more bus driving jobs will be available in the twenty-first century as demand for public transportation increases due to the growing school-age population and to environmental concerns. In recent years, many employers have had difficulty in finding qualified candidates to fill positions. In the future, the best opportunities will be for school bus driving jobs. However, employment of local and intercity drivers will increase as bus ridership grows.

The Job of School Bus Driver

School bus drivers usually work only during the school year. Very few are employed during the summer or school holidays. Some drivers take on the additional job of driving students on field trips or to athletic events. School bus drivers work a split schedule in which they run a morning route to get students to school and an afternoon run to return the students to their homes. Some drivers may run a midday route to drop off and pick up kindergartners who are on a half-day schedule. It may be possible for school bus drivers to take their buses home with them instead of having to return the buses to a terminal or garage.

On the job, school bus drivers must be extremely cautious when children are getting on or off the bus. Plus, they must be able to control the children and enforce the safety rules as well as student conduct rules put in place by the school system. Another task is the preparation of weekly reports on the number of students transported, number of runs completed, and the amount of fuel used on their routes. A supervisor sets time schedules and routes.

How to Become a School Bus Driver

You will need to get a commercial driver's license in order to drive a school bus. Expect also to take some training in driving a bus unless you have had experience driving vehicles larger than an automobile. Most school bus drivers complete between one and four weeks of driving instruction plus classroom training on state and local laws, regulations, and policies of operating school buses. In addition, they study safe driving practices, driver-pupil relations, first aid, the special needs of disabled students, and emergency evacuation procedures. School bus drivers must also learn about school system rules for discipline and conduct for bus drivers and the students they transport.

Job Outlook and Earnings

You won't find it too difficult to get a job as a school bus driver because these jobs are usually plentiful due to their part-time status, the high turnover rate, and the minimal training requirements. In fact, you can expect more job openings to occur in the future as enrollment is predicted to grow in both elementary and secondary schools. Opportunities will be best in suburban areas where students generally ride school buses.

The average earnings for school bus drivers are about $10 per hour. What you make will vary by where you are employed. Some drivers earn less than $6 per hour, and others earn more than $14 per hour. Because bus drivers do not work when school is not in session, they do not get vacation leave. However, they usually receive sick leave, and many are covered by health and life insurance and pension plans.

On the Job with a School Bus Driver

Debbie Walton became interested in driving a school bus when she had two school-aged children. The idea of driving a bus worked well around their schedule. She drove from 7:00 to 9:30 A.M. and from noon or 1:00 to 5:00 P.M. Debbie drove children ranging in age from kindergartners through high school students and was responsible for their safe transport to and from school. She really enjoyed the kids on her route; however, she disliked the split schedule.

Each morning before starting her bus route, Debbie would make a safety inspection of the bus by checking the lights, windshield wipers, tire pressure, brakes, and flashers. She would carefully inspect the bus from front to back. At first, Debbie used a checklist during her inspection. With experience, she relied less on the checklist during her daily inspection. At the end of the day, Debbie bled the brakes, swept the bus, and turned articles left on the bus into the lost and found.

Training to Be a Driver

Debbie had to have a Class B license in her state in order to drive a school bus. She spent ten hours in a classroom learning the ins and outs of driving a school bus and some basic first aid. Then she had to pass a written test over what she had learned in the classroom. Next, an instructor taught her how to drive a bus. This included learning how to bleed the brakes and complete the bus safety checklist used before and after school bus routes. Finally, Debbie had to pass a road test.

Driving a Special-Education School Bus

Janet Hively comes from a family of school bus drivers. Her father and sister have more than forty years of experience between them. It was her sister who told her about the position of driver for special-education students for a rural school corporation. When Janet started this job, she transported preschoolers to and from school; however, the program has steadily grown as more special-education students have been included in regular classrooms. Janet's passengers are now children from preschoolers through high school students who have a wide range of disabilities.

Janet's workday usually begins at about 6:15 A.M., when she does a pretrip check of her fifteen-passenger bus. She checks the oil, lights, tires, and flashers to be sure everything is in proper working order. Then Janet lets the bus warm up for about ten minutes before starting her 150-mile route so that it will be comfortable for the students.

On her first trip of the day, the bus is almost full because Janet drives thirteen students. Five are in wheelchairs and require the use of the wheelchair lift built into the bus. Susie, who has been her aide for several years, helps secure the students into the wheelchair section of the bus or into their seats—a task that can take up to five minutes for each student. This first riders are all dropped off at their different schools by 8:30 A.M. Next, Janet picks up nine preschoolers who have a variety of disabilities requiring Susie's help to seat them. After delivering the preschoolers to the school, Janet has a break for about forty minutes. She may use this time to check the bus for any problems before picking up one student who is only able to attend high school for two hours. After transporting this student to his home, it is time to pick up the preschoolers and return them to their homes. This run takes about forty-five minutes to complete.

For her last run of the day, Janet picks up the children from her first run and takes them to their homes. After dropping off the last rider, Janet checks every seat to be sure no children are still on board. Then, in preparation for the next day, she refuels her bus.

Training for the Job

Before Janet began driving this special-education route, she had to get her commercial driver's license. First, she attended a state-mandated two-week training session. Then she rode with another driver for twelve hours, followed by twelve hours of driving with an instructor on board. Today, new drivers must complete a visual test in which they are required to identify forty points on the bus. They also must be able to identify and name parts such as the transmission, brake lines, air filter, and oil filter. This is to ensure that drivers are able to accurately communicate mechanical problems to supervisors and mechanics.

Janet has received special training in administering CPR as well as instruction in basic sign language so that she can communicate with the deaf children she transports. She has also been trained to help children who are on oxygen, have feeding tubes, or wear heart monitors. Some of this training is a result of her own initiative because it was not required by the school district. Janet believes in going the extra mile for her special passengers.

Career Pluses and Minuses

Janet finds the pay and insurance and retirement benefits offered by her employer to be good. The real plus of her career, however, is getting to know the children and their parents. Janet gives the children a great deal of attention in order to make them feel safe on her bus. As a result, a special bond has developed. Recently, Janet's family had a birthday party for her and several of the students and their families attended the celebration. Most school bus drivers will not have the opportunity to know their riders this well.

This job has also given Janet a great rapport with the teachers of the children she transports. One teacher, especially, has given her solid advice on how to handle these special children effectively when they are riding on her bus. Janet believes that the teachers have made her a better bus driver.

Along with the positive aspects of this job are the negative ones. The weather can make the roads very dangerous and difficult to drive. Then there are the discourteous and reckless drivers, especially those who don't want to get stuck behind a bus, who make her job far more difficult. There is also the difficult situation that arises when one of the children loses control of his or her bodily functions.

The Job of Local Transit Bus Driver

Local transit bus drivers drive buses within a city or suburban area. They begin their workdays by reporting to a terminal or garage where they stock up on all the supplies, such as tickets, transfers, and trip report forms, needed on the job. Few bus drivers now carry money, as passengers are expected to have the correct fare. Some local drivers may have to do a pretrip check of the bus to be sure it is safe to operate before going out on the route. And a few are responsible for making sure that their buses are clean, from washing the windows to cleaning the interior of the bus.

As a local transit driver, you would follow a regularly scheduled route and make several trips along the route during your shift. You may need to stop every few blocks to pick up and discharge passengers. Local bus drivers are also expected to be at stops at the times printed in the official company schedule. This can be extremely difficult because of traffic, weather, problems with passengers, and mechanical breakdowns.

As you drive along your route, you will dispense tickets and transfers and may collects fares. You will also need to be knowledgeable about where passengers need to get off to go to businesses, parks, and other attractions. Furthermore, passengers will expect you to know what buses they need to take to get to different locations. Besides these tasks, you will have to deal with passengers who are frail, unruly, or rude. At the same time, you are responsible for giving everyone from schoolchildren to senior citizens a safe trip. At the end of your workday, you will need to submit reports about the number of trips made, route delays, mechanical difficulties, accidents, and any other problems that occurred.

Like school bus drivers, most local transit bus drivers have a regular work schedule. They usually work a five-day, forty-hour workweek. Some drivers may have to work weekends, evening shifts, or even after midnight. It also may be necessary for drivers to work a split shift, such as 6:00 A.M. to 10:00 A.M. and 3:00 P.M. to 7:00 or 8:00 P.M., in order to accommodate high ridership during commuter rush hours.

Qualifications and Training

Local transit bus companies look for drivers who are at least twenty-four years old, have a high school diploma, are able to read complex bus schedules, and have some previous bus or truck driving experience. A good driver will have excellent customer service skills, be courteous, communicate well with the passengers, and able to manage a large group of people.

Local transit bus drivers must hold a commercial driver's license. Many companies offer training for their new drivers. This usually includes several weeks of classroom work with instruction in reading schedules, keeping records, and dealing with passengers in a professional manner. The behind-the-wheel training typically involves practicing maneuvers such as backing up, changing lanes, and turning. This is first done on a closed course and then later on the highway or streets. Drivers may also make trial runs without passengers to improve their driving skills and learn the routes. In smaller cities, trainees memorize and drive each of the runs operating out of their assigned garages. After completing their training, new drivers may be placed on a call-in status and have to work at any given time, especially on short notice. They are often assigned only part-time hours until they gain experience. As drivers get more seniority, they may be able to request more appealing routes as well as schedules with weekends off and more or less work hours.

Job Outlook and Earnings

You should not have too much difficulty in finding a job as a local transit bus driver because many companies continue to have problems in filling this position. There is some competition for positions that offer regular hours and steady driving routes. Only in a few areas where there are high wages and very attractive benefits is there intense competition for local bus driver jobs.

How much money you make as a local bus driver depends greatly on where you live. The larger the city, the more you will earn. In cities with more than two million inhabitants, you can expect a top hourly income of about $18. In areas with between a quarter million and half a million inhabitants, top hourly wages will be closer to $15. However, in areas with fewer than fifty thousand residents, top hourly wages can be less than $13. Local drivers are usually able to reach the top rate in three or four years.

Driving a Local Transit Bus

After beginning her bus driving career as a school bus driver, Debbie Walton switched to driving a thirty-foot shuttle bus for a small company in a Northern California city that had seven routes and twenty-three drivers. Before she was hired, Debbie had to demonstrate her driving skills. She feels that it was experience that helped her get this job at a time when there was considerable competition for these jobs. After she was hired, a trainer drove with her once to familiarize her with the route she would drive and that was all the training she received. Debbie used street guides to help her out when she first began to drive for this company.

Several years after Debbie got this job, the bus company acquired another company that served adjoining suburban cities. Debbie and the other drivers became the senior drivers and trained incoming drivers to familiarize them with new routes. Over the years, the company became a regional bus system, so many routes became longer, and special routes were created for the commute hours that only ran to the regional transportation trains.

The drivers in this company bid for routes based on seniority. This is a common practice in most local transit companies. Because Debbie is one of the most senior drivers, she is usually able to get the routes she wants. Her preference is to start early in the day and work ten-hour shifts only four days a week. Most of the drivers work eight-hour days, five days a week. Seniority keeps Debbie from having to work weekends. If she does work more than forty hours per week, she is paid time and a half.

A Typical Day on a Route

Because Debbie likes to drive early in the day, she may report to work as early as 4:40 A.M. Before her first route begins at 5:00 A.M., Debbie checks the bus over carefully to make sure it is road safe. This includes bleeding the brakes and checking the brake pressure. She also checks the lights, windshield wipers, tires, and the fire extinguisher. Finally, she does a walk-around, looking over the entire bus. Then this road warrior is ready to roll.

Out on the route, Debbie doesn't handle any money; passengers just put their coins or bills in the fare box. Although she doesn't have an official break, at the end of each loop she usually has five to ten minutes depending on the traffic. Occasionally, she will have fifteen minutes. This is her time to grab a bite to eat. Then it's back on the road again. If Debbie's day begins at 4:40 A.M., it could end as early as 2:40 P.M., when she takes her bus back to headquarters. Then she turns the bus over to the next driver, who checks it out completely before taking it out on the road again. Debbie also hands in her trip card—a record of the hours she worked and the number of people who have ridden the bus.

Career Pluses and Minuses

Debbie appreciates that her job offers good benefits, including medical and dental insurance, paid vacations, and retirement. On the job, she likes being on her own for the entire workday as well as seeing her regular passengers each day. Of course, there are negatives to this job, such as being stuck in traffic, dealing with passengers who don't have fares, worrying that an unsteady older passenger will fall, and not always having a break between runs. One of her biggest challenges is trying to give directions to people who have limited English skills. Sometimes the stress of always being on guard while driving can get to Debbie.

The Job of Intercity Bus Driver

Intercity bus drivers transport passengers from city to city within a state or between different regions of the country. They may make only a single one-way trip to a distant city or a round-trip between cities each day. Drivers may stop at several small towns that are just a few miles apart or stop at large cities that are hundreds of miles apart. While some intercity drivers have extended trips of more than one day, there are strict federal guidelines limiting actual driving time. For instance, long-distance drivers may not work more than sixty hours in a seven-day period and for every ten hours of driving they must rest eight hours.

Intercity drivers work nights, weekends, and holidays and may spend nights away from home at company expense. Drivers with more seniority often have more regular hours during a week; others must be prepared to drive on short notice. Because intercity bus travel service tends to be seasonal, drivers can expect to work as many hours as regulations allow from May through August. During the off-season, some drivers with less seniority may get very few hours. They may even be furloughed and get no driving jobs for a period of time.

Qualifications and Training

Intercity bus companies look for their drivers to have very similar qualifications to those of local transit drivers, including holding a commercial driver's license. Many intercity bus companies offer training for their new drivers. This usually includes two to eight weeks of classroom work and behind-the-wheel training. In the classroom, new drivers will learn U.S. Department of Transportation and company rules, safety regulations, state and municipal driving regulations, and safe driving practices. They also learn how to handle record keeping and the appropriate way to deal with passengers.

Job Outlook and Earnings

Employment opportunities will be best for new intercity bus drivers who have driving experience. Because travelers often opt to make longer trips by plane or rail, employment will only increase as ridership does. Most growth in employment for intercity drivers will probably be in group charter travel, rather than scheduled intercity bus services.

The average hourly pay for intercity bus drivers is slightly better than that of local bus drivers. Their benefits may include paid health and life insurance, sick leave, and free bus rides on any of the routes of their line or system. Full-time drivers may receive as much as four weeks of vacation time annually.

What It's Like to Be an Intercity Bus Driver

As a teenager, Lloyd Benedict liked to drive; however, he never imagined then that he would have a career as a bus driver. Instead, he thought he would become a jeweler. Unfortunately, he soon discovered that he would need a part-time job to supplement his income as a struggling jeweler. He saw an ad for a position as a school bus driver, applied for the job, and got it after attending a two-week course in order to get sufficient training and a license.

After working as a school bus driver for three years, Lloyd decided that he wanted to see more of the country and applied for a job as an intercity driver with Greyhound Lines. When he applied for this job many years ago, the position of driver for Greyhound was held in such high esteem that competition was intense. Only one in forty applicants were hired. Lloyd believes that he was able to get one of these positions because of his three years of experience as a school bus driver and his safe driving record.

After six weeks of company training, Lloyd became a Greyhound driver. Because routes in almost all bus companies are assigned by seniority, Lloyd was placed on the on-call board, which meant he had to be available twenty-four hours a day. He especially remembers being called at night to drive from San Francisco to Reno in a blizzard. As he gained seniority, Lloyd began to be able to choose his runs. His favorite was going from San Francisco to Fort Bragg, California, because it is so scenic. He also traveled frequently to Reno, Fresno, and San Luis Obispo. Most of his routes were completed in a day with only an occasional overnight stay.

As an intercity bus driver, Lloyd felt he had the same role as the captain of a ship. Once he left the bus terminal, he was responsible for everything that happened on the bus. He had to make sure that the passengers behaved in an orderly manner, stop in isolated regions to pick up passengers and collect their fares, as well as load and unload the luggage for the passengers. The company also was a freight carrier, so he had to drop off packages in small towns.

Lloyd drove for Greyhound for seven years. He left this job after a bitter drivers' strike and later began driving a tour bus through the San Francisco Bay Area.

The Job of Motor Coach Driver

Motor coach drivers drive passengers on charter trips and sightseeing tours. Sight-seeing trips can be one-day excursions or extended trips covering several states. Multiday trips will require drivers to be away for several days or possibly several weeks at a time. The hours motor coach drivers spend on the job are dictated by the charter trips booked and the schedule and prearranged itinerary of tours. If you become a motor coach driver, you can expect to work any day and all hours of the day, including weekends and holidays. However, like all bus drivers, your actual hours on the job must be consistent with Department of Transportation rules and regulations.

Qualifications and Training

Motor coach bus drivers must hold a commercial driver's license and comply with the same federal and state regulations as local transit and intercity drivers. A few companies may offer training; however, they usually look for and hire applicants who already have experience driving buses and need very little training.

Job Outlook and Earnings

Driving a charter bus or tour bus tends to be seasonal work, except in popular tourist spots that have visitors throughout the year. Drivers may work the maximum allowable hours during tourist season, which usually runs from May through August. During the off-season, drivers with less seniority may work a limited number of hours and even be furloughed. Motor coach drivers on average will earn less than intercity bus drivers; however, they may also earn tips that substantially increase their incomes.

Driving a Motor Coach in San Francisco

After seven years as a Greyhound driver, Lloyd Benedict, whose career as an intercity driver was described earlier in this chapter, became a tour bus driver. Today, he is the number-two driver for a small tour bus company in San Francisco and is able to select which route he will drive. On most days, he will only work in the city. Occasionally, he will be out of town overnight when he does two- or three-day tours out of San Francisco to Yosemite, Reno, or down the coast to the Monterey Peninsula. He usually drives a very well-appointed forty-foot bus that has a rest room, relieving him of the necessity of making unexpected stops for passengers. The bus has a capacity of fifty to fifty-five passengers; however, groups vary in size and are often smaller.

A Typical Day's Work

Lloyd's day begins when he arrives at the bus yard at 7:45 A.M. He is very familiar with his bus, since he drives the same bus every day. His first task is to prepare and check out the bus. He fuels the bus and does a pretrip check according to a form that he fills out each day. On the day described here, he drove to a hotel where he was to pick up a French tour group at 9:00 A.M. He arrived early and used the time to study for a course that he was taking. Shortly, the guide arrived and talked to him about the sights the tour group would see. Lloyd jotted down the route he would follow once the group was aboard the bus. As the guide described the sights of San Francisco, Lloyd drove by some tourist spots and stopped at others for visits and photo opportunities. At the end of this half-day tour, he drove the group across the Golden Gate Bridge to Sausalito, where the tourists would have lunch before embarking on a ferry ride on the Bay.

Lloyd then returned to San Francisco to pick up another tour group at a hotel to take them to the airport. He loaded their luggage aboard the bus and unloaded it at the airport. Once he left this group, he had some wait time before picking up a new tour group at the airport and taking them to a hotel. Again, he handled the loading and unloading of the luggage by himself. His day was over at this point, and he returned the bus to the company terminal.

Typically, Lloyd works from eight to ten hours a day and drives three or four tour groups around the San Francisco Bay Area. In the high tourist season, which is October, he will work fourteen- to sixteen-hour days six days a week. It is essential for him to do this in order to compensate for the income that he loses during the three or four months when tourism is slack. Although Lloyd works long days, the law prevents him from driving more than ten hours of that time. The rest of the time is wait time, for which he is paid.

Career Pluses and Minuses

The greatest thing about driving a tour bus, according to Lloyd, is that you are working with tourists who are looking forward to having fun. Also, you are able to be home almost every night. This is one career in which you do not have to have more than a high school education and very little training to make a decent living. Lloyd believes that the major negative to this career is the long hours he must work in the high tourist season. It is also becoming increasingly difficult to drive in the traffic of the San Francisco Bay Area.

Driving a Charter Bus in Indiana

Hank Hanson is a driver for the Landmark Charter Coach Service in Fort Wayne, Indiana. While Hank has not always driven buses, he has usually had a career that let him be a road warrior. As a teenager, he drove a milk truck. Then, while he was in the service, Hank was behind the wheel of a truck pulling guns as well as a fuel truck. Hank has also been a driver for a short-haul trucking company and later became its terminal manager, overseeing forty-five drivers. After leaving the trucking company, Hank started a trash collection business, which he built into a successful multitruck operation.

In the back of his mind, Hank never relinquished his boyhood dream of driving a bus. An unexpected delay in a Greyhound bus station gave him the opportunity to begin pursuing this dream. He saw an ad for a job as a Greyhound bus driver and decided to apply. Hank filled out an application, was accepted, and soon was attending a six-week company driving school. After completing the training, he began driving for Greyhound. He didn't have a regular route but was on an extra board, which meant that he could be called at any time to drive. After a short stint as a Greyhound driver, Hank moved to a job with a small four-bus company driving charters.

Working with a Charter Bus Company

Besides driving charter routes for Landmark Charter Coach Service, Hank is the company's safety supervisor. In this role, he takes prospective drivers out in a bus and grades how they drive, looking at how they handle turns and drive on city streets and interstates. A high grade will earn drivers a recommendation for employment. Hank knows the buses very well and frequently helps the company owner solve mechanical problems reported by drivers. Together, they keep this small fleet of buses running and on the road. Landmark currently has one fifty-seven-passenger bus, two forty-seven-passenger buses, and one thirty-five-passenger bus. In addition, Hank attends seminars given by bus manufacturers to learn more about handling new buses and making repairs.

When Hank goes out on the road with a charter, there are usually about forty people in the group. Most of his trips are short runs completed in one day. His longest charter was a nineteen-day tour of the western half of the United States. The group visited places like Yellowstone in Wyoming and the Badlands in South Dakota. He also traveled with the United States Women's Volleyball Team for fourteen days.

In his job as a charter bus driver, Hank takes many senior citizen groups on one-day trips within the state. He also transports many groups to sporting events and frequently drives high school, college, and professional sport teams to their games. Occasionally, Hank will drive a charter for celebrities and has had both Marie Osmond and the Beach Boys aboard his bus.

A Typical Charter Trip for Hank

When Hank drives a tour group on a one-day trip, he will get his bus at the company's terminal, or it will be delivered to him by one of the company's other drivers. Most groups will have an escort who will meet with him to discuss the route and time schedule. On the bus, the escort will oversee the group's activities.

For a one-day charter trip of four hundred miles round-trip to a specialty basket manufacturing and sales company in Ohio, Hank began driving at about 6:00 A.M. The group reached its destination at about 9:00 A.M. Then he transported some of the group to a nearby town for additional touring. Most of the time between a charter's arrival and departure at a destination is downtime for Hank, although the group escort may invite him to go with the group on the planned activity. Usually, he stays with the bus in case anyone in the group requires transportation to a special destination. Hank may use this time to nap because his day can be very long. During the return trip, the Ohio group stopped at a restaurant for dinner, and the trip was not completed until 10:00 P.M.

Career Pluses and Minuses

Hank really enjoys driving and traveling with charter groups. While he used to do more long-distance driving, he now drives shorter one-day trips and still sees lots of great things within the area. He especially enjoys talking with the passengers and getting to know them as they travel. His favorite trip is a tour to Branson, Missouri. On this trip, he joins with the group in attending shows. Then he enjoys the added fun after the shows when the performers frequently get on the bus to greet and talk with the tour. Hank has also had some unpleasant experiences when people on charters have engaged in fights that have actually damaged the bus.

For More Information

In order to learn more about jobs for bus drivers in your area, contact local transit systems, intercity bus lines, school systems, and the local office of the state employment service. You also should check the classified ads in newspapers.

General information on bus driving is available from:

American Bus Association
1100 New York Avenue NW, Suite 1050
Washington, DC 20005
www.buses.org

For school information contact:

National School Transportation Association
P.O. Box 2639
Springfield, VA 22152
www.schooltrans.com

Local transit bus driving information can be obtained from:

American Public Transit Association
1201 New York Avenue NW, Suite 400
Washington, DC 20005
www.apta.com

You can learn about driving a motor coach from:

United Motorcoach Association
113 South West Street, Fourth Floor
Alexandria, VA 22314
www.uma.org

CHAPTER SIX

Careers with Delivery Services

*E*very week, billions of pieces of mail and millions of packages are delivered to homes, offices, and businesses by the United States Postal Service and local, national, and international delivery services. It doesn't matter whether it is a weekday or the weekend or even what time it is, mail and packages are always being delivered. Your local mail carrier leaves letters, bills, advertisements, and packages at your home. Delivery companies pick up letters, documents, and packages from drop boxes, businesses, and residences, then deliver them to addresses across town and almost everywhere in the United States and throughout the world. And messengers in cities often drive deliveries to their destinations in less than an hour.

A career with a delivery service is a good choice for anyone who wants to be on the move throughout the day. While not all of these careers involve driving, a great number do. Mail carriers drive routes in the suburbs and rural areas of the country. Almost every employee of a delivery service who makes deliveries is driving a car, van, or truck. Within this career arena, you can find jobs with the U.S. Postal Service, with giant national and international delivery companies such as FedEx, UPS, DHL, and Airborne Express, and with local delivery and messenger services.

The United States Postal Service

A postal service was created by the Continental Congress in 1775, and Benjamin Franklin was appointed the first postmaster general. Prior to that time, the postal service was a monopoly run by an appointee of the King of England. The colonists were very unhappy with this system, as their mail could be opened and read to check their loyalty to the crown. When the Continental Congress established a mail service in 1782, it was decreed that private letters could not be opened by the postal authorities. Then in 1789, Congress passed the first postal act establishing the Post Office Department. This department was replaced with the United States Postal Service as an independent government agency in 1971 in order to provide the country with a more efficient and timely mail service. To accomplish this task, the postal service now employs about nine hundred thousand employees. If you want to be on the move delivering mail, you could be one of these workers.

The Job of Mail Carrier

Mail carriers cover their routes on foot, by vehicle, or a combination of both. In some urban and most rural areas, they use a car or small truck. Although the postal service provides vehicles to city carriers, most rural carriers have to use their own automobiles.

The carriers do far more than deliver mail: they also collect money for postage-due and COD (cash on delivery) fees, and they obtain signed receipts for registered, certified, and insured mail. If you become a city carrier, you could also have very specialized duties. You might deliver only certain types of mail or just pick up mail from mail collection boxes. As a rural carrier, you should expect to provide a wider variety of services than city carriers. These carriers may sell stamps and money orders and register, certify, and insure parcels and letters.

Mail carriers usually begin their days in the post office, where they arrange the mail in delivery sequence. Fortunately, automated equipment has reduced sorting time, allowing carriers to spend more time out on their routes delivering mail. At the end of the day, drivers of postal vehicles will return them to the post office.

Work Conditions for Mail Carriers

It is not always easy to be a mail carrier. They frequently have to work overtime during peak delivery times, such as before the winter holidays. Their regular week, however, is forty hours over a five-day period. Carriers also have to deliver mail in all kinds of weather, from cold, snowy winter days to hot summer days. Plus, driving a postal vehicle requires the driver to do stop-and-start driving and to watch very carefully for other drivers and pedestrians, especially before and after making deliveries. There is also considerable reaching in this job in order to get the mail from postal vehicles into every box on the route. And at times, mail carriers need to leave their vehicles in order to deliver the mail to certain addresses. While carriers often begin work early in the morning, they have the advantage of being through by early afternoon. Most mail carriers particularly like having a job in which their workdays are relatively free of direct supervision.

Job Qualifications

To become a mail carrier, you must be at least eighteen years old and a United States citizen or have been granted permanent resident-alien status. Qualification for the job is based on a written examination that measures speed and accuracy at checking names and numbers and the ability to memorize mail distribution procedures. You must also pass a physical examination and may be asked to show that you can lift and handle mail sacks weighing seventy pounds. In addition, you need to have a driver's license, a good driving record, and receive a passing grade on a road test.

In order to begin the process of becoming a mail carrier, you need to contact the post office or mail processing center where you want to work to find out when an examination will be given. After an examination, all of the applicants' names are listed in order of their examination scores. Veterans who were honorably discharged have five additional points added to their scores and those who were wounded in combat or are disabled have ten additional points added. When a vacancy occurs, the appointing officer chooses one of the top three applicants; the rest of the names remain on the list to be considered for future openings until their eligibility expires—usually two years after the examination date.

Training

As a mail carrier, you can expect to be trained on the job by experienced workers. Many post offices offer classroom instruction on safety and defensive driving. Whenever new equipment or procedures are introduced, you will receive additional instruction from another postal worker or a training specialist.

Advancement

Mail carriers often begin on a part-time, flexible basis and become regular or full-time in order of seniority as vacancies occur. Carriers can look forward to obtaining preferred routes as their seniority increases or to getting high-level jobs, such as carrier technician. They can advance to supervisory positions on a competitive basis.

Job Outlook

It is very important to understand that there is keen competition for jobs as mail carriers because the number of applicants always exceeds the number of openings. Although mail volume will increase and partnership with express delivery companies will increase the volume of mail to be delivered, several trends are expected to increase carrier productivity and lead to slower than average growth for these workers. The increased use of the "delivery point sequencing" system, which allows machines to sort mail directly to the order of delivery, should decrease the amount of time carriers spend sorting the mail, allowing them more time to handle long routes. Plus, the postal service is moving toward more centralized mail delivery, such as the increased use of cluster boxes, to cut down on the number of door-to-door deliveries.

The Earnings Picture

The median annual earnings of mail carriers exceed $35,000. The middle 50 percent earn between $30,000 and $38,000. The lowest 10 percent will have earnings of less than $26,000, while the top 10 percent earn more than $40,000. Mail carriers enjoy a variety of employer-provided benefits similar to those enjoyed by other federal government workers.

A Career as a Mail Carrier

Selina Lodge delivers mail in a suburban area that features widely spaced homes perched on hills as well as on level ground. It is a rather solitary route. Selina drives a small half-ton truck and has to be extremely cautious because the roads are narrow and the hills are steep. Since her first day as a carrier, she has always had the same route. Although this route was her third choice, she now feels very strongly that she lucked out.

Like so many other carriers, Selina did not start her career with the postal service working in this position. Instead, she started as a scheme clerk working from midnight to 8:30 A.M. in a general mail facility. Scheme clerks have the task of keying a code on every letter that passes by them so that it can be routed correctly. Selina had to glance at a letter and then instantly decide whether to designate it as state mail, foreign mail, military mail, San Francisco mail, or mail for another San Francisco Bay area city. She remained in this job for several years until she became a mail carrier.

Becoming a Carrier

In order for Selina to become a carrier, she was required to get a U.S. Department of Transportation license. To qualify for this license, she had to have a good driving record, possess a state driver's license, pass a physical, and be an insured driver. If she gets too many speeding or traffic violations on her state driver's license, she could be suspended or even lose her job.

Selina was trained for a full day on the Jeep that she would drive on her route. An instructor showed her how to drive the vehicle and then tested her driving skills in an open lot where she had to maneuver through cones. Since then, she has gone through the same training for the other two vehicles that she has driven on the route.

On the Job

Selina starts her job at 7:15 A.M. after checking in on the computerized job clock. Then, she picks up her keys and goes out to inspect her vehicle for any possible problems. Next, it's back to the post office to spend close to three hours sorting mail into cases in the exact order of her route. Because she has a high-volume route that includes about four hundred customers, she will sort from ten to fourteen feet of letters and flats (magazines and manila envelopes). Every letter will have to be placed in the correct spot in one of the cases that will go in her truck. Selina also has to indicate the addresses on the route where she will be dropping off packages.

Once all the sorting is completed, and it does have to be done rapidly, Selina puts all the mail and packages in a hamper and rolls them out to her truck and loads it. Then it's time to drive out to her route and begin delivering the mail. The route is nearly twenty miles long and takes about five and a half hours to complete. Selina will drive about five miles per hour between homes. She only increases her speed when she needs extra momentum to climb the hills.

At each stop, Selina will need to finger through several cases to be sure she has all the letters, magazines, advertisements, and packages for that address. She has developed a system to this work that enables her to deliver the mail quickly. (Each carrier will devise a system that works the easiest for him or her.) While most of her workday on the route is spent driving, Selina frequently will have to jump out of the truck to leave a package at a door.

Also, she often takes the time to provide extra services for a few of the elderly people on her route, who truly appreciate her helpfulness. When she has completed her route, Selina will return to the post office. If she has not worked eight hours, she will usually case bulk mail until she has.

A Good Job

Selina is pleased that she has stayed on the same route for so many years. She knows many of the people on the route and finds them to be polite and friendly. It is also fun to wave or talk to the other delivery people who regularly make deliveries to homes along her route. Like Selina, many of them have had the same route for several years. Not only does she like driving, she also likes being independent and working without a boss looking over her shoulder. There is also the added benefit of driving a very scenic route where she can enjoy the changing of the seasons and delight in the decorations her customers place on their homes.

Selina is a very safe driver. She has never had an accident, broken a side mirror, hit a mailbox, or had a moving violation. She finds being a mail carrier an ideal job for people who love to be behind the wheel. This road warrior plans to be delivering mail for many years to come.

Large Express Transportation Companies

As commerce expanded in the twentieth century, a demand arose for delivery services beyond what the post office offered. Stores needed to have goods picked up and then delivered to customer homes; businesses wanted documents, packages, and freight to be picked up at their workplaces and delivered as quickly as possible to other businesses; and many people wanted to have mail and packages brought to their homes overnight. This demand for quick service, coupled with pickup and delivery, spawned the development of large express transportation companies that now offer overnight delivery to most areas in the United States as well as abroad. Today, these companies have developed extremely sophisticated delivery systems. However, at the heart of all these systems is a driver of a delivery truck who initially picks up a shipment and another driver who will deliver it to a customer who may be ten or three thousand miles away. Within every one of these large companies, there are thousands of positions for road warriors who want to spend their days on the move.

Airborne Express

Back in 1946, Airborne Flower Traffic Association of California was founded to fly fresh flowers to the mainland from Hawaii. After several mergers, Airborne Express emerged between 1979 and 1981. The company's mission is to provide businesses with customized distribution solutions that include such services as overnight, next-afternoon, and second-day delivery and same-day courier service. In 2000, the company handled more than three hundred million domestic shipments and more than six million international shipments. The company employs many drivers who want to be on the move every day—it has more than fifteen thousand delivery vehicles.

FedEx

Founder Frederick W. Smith started FedEx to overcome the tremendous problems that existed in 1971 in getting packages and other airfreight delivered within a day or two. On its first night of operation, the company delivered 186 packages to twenty-five cities in the United States; by 2001, it was delivering about 3.3 million packages and documents every night and more than seven million pounds of freight. The company also served more than two hundred countries around the world and had more than 45,500 vehicles for drivers working for this company to drive.

DHL

Three California entrepreneurs (Adrian Dalsey, Larry Hillblom, and Robert Lynn) formed DHL in 1969 as a service between San Francisco and Hawaii. The company rapidly grew, initiating service to the Philippines, Japan, Hong Kong, and other destinations in the Pacific Basin. This was followed by expansion to Europe, Latin America, the Middle East, and Africa. In 1986, DHL was the first company to bring international air express services to the People's Republic of China. By 1999, the company had an approximate 40 percent market share of international express traffic and was delivering 160 million shipments per year.

UPS

Nineteen-year-old Jim Casey borrowed $100 from a friend in 1907 to start the American Messenger Company, which he ran with other teenagers and his brother. The company specialized in delivering packages for retail stores. In 1919, the company, which had earlier merged with a competitor, became known as United Parcel Service. In the 1950s, the company began expanding beyond delivering for retail stores to become a giant delivery service. By 2001, it was handling more than 12.9 million packages and documents a day. All of the senior management of UPS began their careers as package sorters, drivers, or administrative assistants.

What It's Like to Drive for UPS

While Shane Barlow was still in college, he began his career with UPS loading delivery trucks. He would work full-time at this job, which began at 3:30 in the morning, and then attend college at night. Because this job pays well, many college students work as loaders and then go on to other positions in the company. UPS likes to promote workers within the company because they already know so much about how it operates. After several years of loading trucks, Shane had the opportunity to become a part-time driver substituting for regular drivers. His experience as a loader helped him get this job because he knew how to place shipments within a truck. Shane's day as a substitute driver would begin at 8:30 in the morning after he had finished his job as a loader, and his job might not end until 5:30 or 6:30 in the evening. Sometimes, he would work a fourteen- or fifteen-hour day.

To become a UPS driver, Shane needed to obtain a Department of Transportation card. To get this card, he had to have a regular driver's license and a clean driving record and to pass a physical examination. He also had to demonstrate to the company that he could lift 150 pounds using a handcart and could move reasonably fast. Once Shane was approved as a driver, he was given three days of training.

Driving a Regular Route

Before Shane graduated from college, he had become a full-time driver with UPS. At first, he did not have a regular route and floated between different routes. However, as he gained seniority, he bid for the route that he has today. There are 105 drivers on routes working out of the center where he begins and ends his day. Shane's route is primarily in a residential area in a suburb; however, he also stops at a few businesses. He has been on this route for several years. In a day, he will drive from fifty-five to seventy-five miles.

Between 8:00 and 8:15 A.M., Shane's delivery truck is loaded. All the deliveries that must be made before 10:30 A.M. are placed up front in the cab. Shane immediately looks at them and decides on the best possible route to ensure that these shipments are delivered on time. After completing these deliveries, he looks at the other shipments and redoes the shelves so that each delivery can easily be found as he starts out on his route. He has found that the same addresses tend to get most of the deliveries. At each delivery stop, Shane has to be very careful that the truck is safely parked. Then he finds the right shipment, scans it into a handheld computer, exits the truck on the right side, and makes the delivery. Most shipments are simply left at the door. For a few, he needs to record signatures electronically. When he returns to the truck, Shane enters into the computer pertinent facts about the delivery so that UPS will have an accurate record of when, where, and to whom the shipment was delivered. Rather than having to type in most of this data, he simply presses certain buttons on the computer.

During the course of the workday, Shane will make from 170 to 190 delivery stops and approximately five to ten pickups that have been called in. Some drivers whose routes are in more densely populated areas will only make seventy to ninety stops a day but will deliver more pieces than Shane does. Drivers who

deliver primarily to businesses may also stop at the same addresses every day to pick up shipments.

When Shane has delivered every package on his truck, he
returns the vehicle to the hub. A day may end as early as 4:00
P.M. or as late as 9:30 P.M. Throughout the day, he has been on
the move. He believes that this career is a good choice for those
who want to spend most of their workday behind the wheel.

Career Advice

Shane wants prospective drivers to understand that this career
involves hard work. He points out that drivers must be energetic
as deliveries need to be made quickly. Plus, days can be long
because drivers are expected to finish their routes, so working
overtime is part of the job. Besides being a safe driver, Shane says
it is very important for drivers to have a good sense of direction.

Local and Regional Delivery Services

The job of delivering documents, packages, and freight is not just
handled by national and international delivery services and the
postal service. Most larger cities have a number of small to mid-
size companies that pick up and make deliveries within the city
or throughout a region. Much of their work involves same-day or
overnight pickup and delivery. They also deliver shipments to airports and pick up shipments at the airport for delivery. A few
offer additional services, such as crating and storage. These companies give road warriors the opportunity to drive trucks, vans,
pickups, and cars in both full-time and part-time jobs.

Bay Area Delivery

The goal of Bay Area Delivery in Concord, California, is to "cre-
ate dependability and confidence with your deliveries." The

company offers very speedy delivery; most of the shipments that its drivers pick up are delivered on the same day. It handles items that weigh from one to one thousand pounds in an area extending from the state capital of Sacramento to Santa Cruz on the Pacific Ocean (a distance of about 150 miles). The company has a courier component that delivers documents and packages and a freight side that delivers kitchen cabinets to homes that are being built or remodeled.

Delivery work is always done at a fast pace and can be exciting, especially when there is a medical emergency and the driver has to pick up a part for a CAT scanner and rush it to the airport to catch a certain flight. Of course, every day there is last-minute work, especially from graphic artists who want to get their work to customers by the end of the business day.

Bay Area Delivery is owned by Robert and Pat Clarenbach. He works in the office eight to ten hours a day dispatching drivers and handling the paperwork. This is an on-time, on-call business that operates around the clock, 365 days a year. When Robert leaves the office, the business goes with him, as the phone rings in his home. The busiest time of the day for the company is between 8:00 A.M. and 2:00 P.M., as 90 percent of the calls come in during this time. Then there will be a minirush of calls between 3:30 P.M. and 5:00 P.M. each afternoon. When a call comes in, one of the dispatchers will answer it, write down the delivery details, and dispatch a driver to the location for the pickup. They communicate with the drivers by pagers, phones, and two-way radios.

Working as a Driver

The drivers who deliver documents and packages for Bay Area Delivery can hang around the office waiting for an assignment, but most are at home or in their own cars, pickups, and vans or in company vehicles handling deliveries or waiting for another job assignment. These drivers typically start their workdays between 7:30 A.M. and 8:00 A.M. and are usually done by 2:00 P.M. However, because they work for a company that operates twenty-four hours a day, they may make deliveries at all hours of the day and night. On an average day, a driver will travel between 80 to 120 miles. Besides driving, the drivers have to load and unload the shipments and complete paperwork at each stop. This is a job in which individual drivers have a great deal of freedom. They choose the routes that they take to make deliveries and can usually take time off when they wish. The drivers are paid an hourly rate and are reimbursed if they use their own vehicles. For the road warriors who do not wish to drive a regular route, this job presents an opportunity to travel to different areas each day.

Company drivers who work on the freight side of this delivery company will work each day from 7:30 A.M. to 4:00 P.M. driving twenty-four-foot trucks. The trucks are loaded in the morning with kitchen cabinets of varying sizes. Then the driver and a helper will make at least four and as many as eight deliveries during the day. Together, they will unload the cabinets at each stop.

Messenger Delivery Services

Local and regional delivery services make some of the same types of deliveries that are done by messenger services. However, messenger services usually concentrate on delivering smaller shipments in a limited area. By sending a shipment by messenger, the sender ensures that it reaches its destination on the same day or within the hour. Typically, messenger services are used to transport original and legal documents, blueprints and other oversize materials, large multipage documents, and securities. They also pick up and deliver medical samples, specimens, and other materials that must be delivered in a hurry.

On the job, messengers receive their instructions either by reporting to their offices in person, by telephone, or by two-way radio. They then pick up the item and carry it to its destination. After a delivery is made, they check with their offices to receive instructions about the next delivery. Consequently, they spend most of the working day in a vehicle, either their own or one the company provides. In some areas, deliveries are made by bicycle or on foot.

Job Outlook and Earnings

Not as many messengers are needed today as in the past because of the widespread use of electronic information-handling technology. For example, fax machines and E-mail allow documents to be sent across town instantly. However, messengers will continue to be needed for the documents that cannot be sent electronically, as well as for packages. For one out of three messengers, this is a part-time job. Also, many messengers are independent contractors.

Messengers who work for delivery services may charge the services a fee for each item they pick up and deliver. Others work by the hour. The average hourly income is more than $8 per hour. Some messengers receive additional income through tips.

For More Information

To get more information about employment as a mail carrier, you should contact your local post office or a state employment service office. They will be able to supply you with details about entrance examinations and specific employment opportunities for mail carriers.

The large express transportation companies have a wealth of information about their companies as well as employment opportunities on their websites. You may wish to visit the following sites:

- Airborne Express: www.airborne.com

- DHL: www.DHL-usa.com/index

- FedEx: www.fedex.com/us

- UPS: www.ups.com

Information about job opportunities for messengers may be obtained from local employers and local offices of the state employment service. Besides working for messenger services, there are jobs for messengers at mail-order firms, banks, printing and publishing firms, utility companies, retail stores, and other large firms.

CHAPTER SEVEN

Careers with Driving Schools

C areers that put you on the move for most of the work-day are not limited to those where you will be doing the driving. Instead, you can be the one teaching others how to drive. You could be employed at a commercial school teaching teenagers how to drive, as this is now the way most learn. Or you could be employed at a company, public, or private school teaching adults how to drive buses and trucks, as few are still learning on the road from experienced drivers. There is also the possibility of teaching people to race or drive professionally at a high-performance driving school. In most of these jobs, you will spend almost all of your time on the move in a vehicle on roads, streets, and highways, and at special training facilities.

Is Teaching Driving Right for You?

Successful driver training instructors share certain attributes that allow them to shine in the profession. Answer the following questions to see if you are like those instructors.

1. Do you like working closely with people? You cannot be a loner in this job.

2. Are you able to assess a person's ability to handle a task? If you can't, you might ask someone to do something that could endanger you and the other person.

3. Can you see what a person needs to do to acquire a certain skill? You must understand the steps involved in learning specific driving skills.

4. Can you give instructions so that they are easily understood and followed? Confused trainees can get in accidents.

5. Can you remain calm in tense situations? All driving teachers will face scary moments.

6. Do you like helping others learn new skills? Good instructors love to teach.

7. Are you an organized person? You need to teach driving according to a well-thought-out lesson plan.

8. Are you patient? Students will not learn at the same rate; some require more instruction.

9. Do you have a good driving safety record? You must be concerned about safety in order to teach it.

10. Are you a skilled driver? You cannot teach skills that you do not have.

If you answered yes to most of these questions and have a good driving record, then a career teaching driving may be one you should explore.

High School Driver Training Programs

In the 1940s and 1950s, it was very common for high schools to offer both driver education classes in the classroom and driver training behind the wheel of a car. Due to a shortage of teachers and funds, the majority of schools now only offer classroom instruction. For example, in California just seven of the one thousand high school districts now have training behind the wheel. There are very few positions for driver training teachers in public schools. Plus, to work at a high school, you need to be a college graduate and have been certified by the state in driver education.

Commercial Driver Training Schools

If you decide on a career teaching people how to drive cars, you will probably work in one of the approximately twenty-five hundred commercial driver training schools in the United States. Most are small and only have three or four cars. Approximately five hundred of the schools have from seven to nine cars, and less than fifty of the schools have more than ten cars. Once you gain experience as a driver training instructor, there is also the possibility of opening your own school and becoming an owner-instructor, as many instructors have done.

The number of hours of classroom and behind-the-wheel instruction time that driving schools offer is based on state law. The most common pattern is thirty classroom hours and six hours driving time. Some instructors teach both in the classroom and cars; however, most will concentrate on one or the other area.

Job Qualifications for Driver Training Instructors

There are separate licenses with different requirements for classroom instructors and driver training instructors. Although requirements for the driver training license may vary between states, you will usually have to be twenty-one years old and a high school graduate, have passed a forty-hour course divided between classroom and behind-the-wheel instruction, possess a clean driving record, have FBI and possibly state clearance, as well as pass both the written and driving parts of the state licensing test. You may also have to pass a physical examination. To even apply for an instructor's license, you will need to be sponsored by a driving school that will hire you after you receive a license. Before you actually begin teaching at a driving school, you can expect the school to give you some on-the-job training.

What It's Like to Be a Driver Training Instructor

Seventy percent of your students will be teenagers; the remainder will be adults, especially those born in other countries. Because most states now have graduated licensing for teenage drivers, your six hours with each of these students are likely to be divided into three separate two-hour sessions. The first session will allow the teens to get a learner's permit. Then after they have driven for twenty-five or thirty hours with a driver who is twenty-five or older, they will take the second two hours. The remaining instruction is given after the students have completed another twenty-five to thirty hours on the road.

Whether you are teaching teenagers or adults, what you teach in each session with a student driver is usually spelled out by your driving school. Of course, you will have to adjust your instruction to the individual drivers as they will not all pick up skills at the same rate. For example, some may need more help with backing or parallel parking, and a few will need very little instruction.

As a driving instructor, you will usually pick each student up at his or her home in a car provided by the school. You will probably be able to take this car home and drive it as your own. The only special equipment that it will have is an additional set of brakes and sometimes a steering wheel on the passenger side for the instructor to use, if necessary.

How much you teach depends on whether you are a full-time or part-time instructor. Some full-time instructors will teach as many as five students in a day (ten hours). Because most of your students will be in high school, your work schedule is largely determined by when they are free. Except in the summer, you can expect your workday to begin after 3:00 P.M. and extend into the evening. You will also work on weekends.

Job Outlook and Earnings

The introduction of the graduated license in most states has increased the number of teenagers who are taking commercial driver training courses. If they take and pass a certified driver training program, they are able to get a driver's license at sixteen; otherwise, they have to wait until eighteen. Since most teens have an overwhelming desire to be on the road behind the wheel, the demand for driver training instructors is increasing.

Driver training instructors in commercial schools are usually paid by the hour. Only a few are salaried employees. Those who use their own cars may contract for work at more than one school. How much you earn in this job depends greatly on where you live as well as the number of hours you work. The average hourly pay for instructors in the United States and Canada is $12. However, if you live in a rural area, you may earn as low as $8 per hour. In some metropolitan areas, driving schools pay as high as $20 per hour. Full-time employees will usually receive health benefits and paid vacations.

The Career Path of a California Driving Instructor of the Year

Before Walter Branch became a driver training instructor, he worked with troubled youth in social service organizations. When he decided to change careers, he knew that he wanted to continue working with young people. He also thought of how he had always enjoyed driving. The possibility of having a career that included both of these elements was realized when he saw an ad for instructors at a large commercial driving school. Before being hired, Walter had to get a state license to become a driver training instructor. The school gave him eighty hours of training split equally between classroom and on-the-road instruction that he needed for a license.

As an instructor at this school, Walter's workday was 9:00 A.M. to 5:00 P.M. In the morning, he would teach adults, and in the afternoon his students were primarily teenagers. He typically worked weekends and had two days off during the week in this job. After Walter amassed a thousand hours of working with students in the car, he was able to obtain a license to teach driver education in the classroom.

Becoming a Driving School Manager

An opportunity arose for Walter to work as a manager and driver training instructor at a driving school that had five cars and five instructors. In his new job, he also started teaching in the classroom. From this school, he moved to a larger school with twenty cars as an instructor and then became the manager. Besides handling the manager's job, Walter also teaches driver education classes in the classroom as well as driver training classes on the road. His many responsibilities include scheduling the other drivers and training all new drivers. Plus, he has to devote time to riding with all the instructors to ensure that they are following the school's driving curriculum. One of the perks of his position is that Walter no longer works on weekends.

On the Road Instructing Students

Because of his many other responsibilities, Walter is only out on the road with students two or three days a week. Like all the other drivers at the school, he follows a prescribed format in each training session. The first two-hour session is designed to acquaint students with the car. They learn such things as how to read the gauges, adjust mirrors, and operate all accessories. Then Walter takes them out on neighborhood streets where they engage in such basics as steering, making right and left turns, and backing up. The second session is devoted to freeway driving, while the third is a review of everything they have learned. During this last session, he pretests them to make sure they have mastered all of the skills essential to passing the state driving license test.

Walter tries to make his driving sessions very practical. If it is time to fuel the car, the student will pump the gas and wash the windows at the service station. At the end of each session, he goes over the student's strengths and weaknesses so the student will know what areas he or she should concentrate on improving before the next session or the state driving test.

Over the years, Walter has had his share of scares. In fact, he doesn't believe that you truly are a driving instructor until you have been scared. He particularly remembers an adult who changed lanes in front of an eighteen-wheeler without his telling her to do so.

Career Satisfactions

Walter is proud that he has driven six hundred thousand miles and taught more than eight thousand students without ever being involved in an accident. He has found it delightful to work with people who are so anxious to learn. Because Walter has taught so many students, he is unable to go anywhere in his community without running into someone he has taught to drive. Walter's expertise as an instructor has been recognized by the Driving School Association of California, which named him the Driving Instructor of the Year.

Truck Driver Training Schools

Throughout the country, there are different types of truck driving schools. You could teach driving at a community college or vocational-technical school and be part of a staff that offers a wide variety of courses. There are also private driving schools as well as schools operated by trucking companies. At each of these schools, the primary course that you should expect to teach is the operation of tractor-trailers. The length of this course is typically more than four weeks, with both classroom instruction and behind-the-wheel practice. Instructors who want to be on the move will opt to teach in the tractor-trailer truck rather than the classroom. In most of these vehicles, seats have been placed in the sleeper area so one or more students can observe the student driver and instructor.

There is one other type of truck driving school where you could teach. These schools are operated by major trucking companies for their newly hired drivers who already know how to drive a tractor-trailer. They are designed to hone their employees' driving skills as well as introduce them to the business side of handling all the paperwork required by the company.

When you investigate job opportunities as an instructor, you should also consider whether or not the school offers entry-level courses that are certified as meeting the minimum standards of the Professional Truck Driver Institute (PTDI). If so, you know that you will be teaching a course that meets the standards set by the industry in curriculum, instruction, behind-the-wheel time, and reputation with funding sources and the industry itself. Appendix B has a list of these schools.

Job Outlook

Each year, the trucking industry needs eighty thousand new drivers. Many of these drivers will need to attend a truck driving school in order to learn how to operate tractor-trailers. Even experienced drivers will need some schooling to learn how to handle each company's nondriving side of trucking, from paperwork to dealing with customers. Demand for truck driving instructors will remain high as long as the demand for truck drivers is high.

Western Pacific Truck School

Western Pacific Truck School has graduated more than twenty thousand successful drivers since it was founded in 1977 in California. Today, the school has seven campuses, five in California and two in Oregon, and employs more than fifty instructors. The quality of its entry-level truck driver training courses has led to this school being certified by the Professional Truck Driver Institute. Each instructor in the school has a minimum of five years of experience behind the wheel.

To become an instructor at this school, it is necessary to have at least five years of successful truck driving experience, as well as to be licensed as a truck driving instructor in California. In order to keep this license, the instructors have to take continuing education courses.

Once someone is hired as an instructor, he or she participates in a forty-hour company training program. Then, to ensure the instructors continually use the highest level of teaching skills, the director of education or a campus manager rides with each instructor every three months to provide additional coaching.

What Is Taught

Although there are other programs, most instructors at Western Pacific teach the Advanced Tractor-Trailer Operator Program, which lasts four and a half weeks. Successful completion allows graduates to receive a diploma and a Class A commercial driver's license, which truck drivers must have to drive on interstate highways and across state lines. It also gives them everything they need to know to get employed in the trucking industry. They also receive a Certificate of Attainment from PTDI. Here is an outline of what is taught in this 180-hour program.

Advanced Tractor-Trailer Operator Program Outline

Orientation

An Introduction to Trucking

Control Systems

Hours of Service for Drivers

Vehicle Inspection

Vehicle Systems

Basic Control

Shifting

Backing

Coupling and Uncoupling

Visual Search

Communication

Space Management

Speed Management

Night Driving

Extreme Driving Conditions

Hazard Awareness

Emergency Maneuvers

Skid Control and Recovery

Accident Procedures

Sliding Fifth Wheels and Tandem Axles

Special Rigs

Preventive Maintenance and Servicing

Recognizing and Reporting Malfunctions

Handling Cargo

Cargo Documentation

Personal Health and Safety

Trip Planning

Public Relations and Employer-Employee Relations

The Commercial Driver's License

Troubleshooting

Classroom Review and Testing

Total Classroom Hours: 110

Total Field Hours: 70

The Instructor's Job

With each class, instructors at Western Pacific Truck School spend sixty hours teaching in an actual classroom. The remaining fifty hours of class time are spent with the equipment (tractor-trailer), teaching such things as how to adjust brakes and couple and uncouple trailers. When students are ready to begin their actual driving experience, two students go with each instructor in a training truck that acts as a rolling classroom. The first sessions are held in the company yard, where the instructor demonstrates such skills as backing up and maneuvering before the students take turns behind the wheel practicing them. Skills are introduced slowly so that they will be completely mastered by the students. When the students are ready, they will venture out on the road to very low-traffic areas to practice shifting and downshifting. While the instructor does not have dual controls, the instructor can reach the brakes on the dash to stop the truck, if necessary. As the students become more skilled drivers, they will drive on the open road in highway, city, and heavy-traffic conditions. By graduation day, each student will have spent seventy hours in the truck, of which forty-four hours are behind the wheel.

Being an instructor at a truck driving school will not give you a great number of hours behind the wheel. However, it will give you the immense satisfaction of helping students take the first steps in becoming professional drivers. It is, therefore, an excellent career choice for road warriors.

The Career Path of an Instructor at a Company Driving School

Instructors at company driving schools are drivers who have proved themselves on the road. During the course of his career, Marty Fortun, an industry-acclaimed driver whose recent career was described in Chapter 4, has worked as an instructor. Interestingly, Marty did not learn to drive a truck by attending a driving school. Instead, he learned from family members and on the job at a very early age. This confirmed road warrior even had a job hauling cattle before graduating from high school; he kept the job for a year after graduation before entering the army. In the army, Marty was able to spend three years as a truck driver and left as a very experienced driver.

After completing his stint with the army, Marty was eager to find a job as a professional truck driver. He was able to get a job driving with Schneider National Carriers, where his father worked as a driver, and has been with the company ever since. At that time, company drivers had to be twenty-three, and he was only twenty-two. However, the company said an exception would be made if he agreed to team with his father.

Because of his great aptitude for truck driving, Marty was given his own truck after just three months of team driving. Then, he spent the next two years driving a refrigerated truck on a local route in California.

A Job as a Training Engineer

At the age of twenty-four, Marty became the youngest training engineer that Schneider National Carriers had ever had who had not attended a driving school. New drivers would attend the Schneider school and then complete their preparation for a career with the company by driving on the road with a training engineer. Marty especially enjoyed this job because the drivers were so eager to get into trucking. He would go out on the road with them, and while they drove he would train them in such things as log writing and trip planning. He would also explain how to handle different situations on the road.

Working as an Instructor

After working as a training engineer for a year, Marty became an instructor at the company's driving school. His job was to hone the actual driving skills of new drivers. On the first day, he would always take students on a demonstration drive so they could see good driving techniques as well as clearly see that he was an experienced driver who knew how to do what he would be teaching them. Then Marty would relinquish the wheel and begin teaching the drivers the basic skills that they would need. This training was done at both the company facility and on the roads around Green Bay, Wisconsin. Part of his time as an instructor was spent working on the skid pad teaching students how to handle skids. The pad had a special surface that became very slippery when water was sprayed on it. He would teach the students both how to get out of skids and how to avoid skidding. When a trailer begins to come around, the driver cannot feel it. Marty had to teach his students to use their mirrors when they were in situations where the truck could jackknife. During the one year that Marty worked at this job, the school would check periodically that he was teaching what they wanted him to teach.

Back on the Road Again

While Marty was working at the company driving school, he met his future wife, Lisa, who was employed in the office. The company wanted all personnel to know more about trucking from the driver's perspective, and she was assigned to ride with him. After they were married, Marty went back to driving, and shortly thereafter Lisa decided to go with him on the road and learn how to become a driver. Because he was an instructor, Marty was able to help Lisa obtain the chauffeur's license, which was all that was needed at that time. Then, every weekend, they would use her father's tractor-trailer so he could teach her how to drive. First, they worked at the company facility and then, on the road. When she was up to Schneider's standards, Lisa took a road test and became a company driver after an additional week of training at the company school. Lisa has become such a good driver that she, like Marty, has received numerous industry awards for her skills.

Their company now has a program in which a driver who has worked for the company for six months can train his or her spouse to become a driver. Throughout the industry, husband and wife driving teams are particularly sought because they are such stable teams. Marty and Lisa are now just one of the many husband and wife teams working in the industry.

High-Performance Driving Schools

Commercial driving schools instruct people in the basics of driving a car so that they can obtain a driver's license. High-performance driving schools take over where they leave off by offering such courses as:

- *Highway Survival*: Teaches car handling skills to those who want to become more confident drivers.

- *Defensive Driving*: Teaches drivers, often teenagers, the skills needed to avoid accidents. Stresses car control techniques, including skid control and advanced braking.

- *High-Performance Driving*: Gives drivers advanced training to increase their enjoyment of driving. Offers advanced driving experiences on a racetrack or specially designed course that cannot be obtained on public highways. Lets drivers use their own cars.

- *Road Racing*: This course is for people who want to know what it is like to drive a race car on a track, for those who want beginning or advanced instruction in driving a race car, as well as for experienced racers.

- *Security Driver Training*: Teaches chauffeurs, security personnel, and executives how to detect, avoid, and deter potentially dangerous situations.

- *Specialty Courses*: Designed to teach stunt drivers and police the skills required in their careers.

High-performance driving schools range in size from the large Bob Bondurant School, which offers a wide variety of courses, to much smaller schools offering a very limited curriculum.

The Bob Bondurant School of High-Performance Driving

More than eighty thousand people have taken courses at the Bondurant School. In this group are movie stars, such as Paul Newman, Clint Eastwood, Tommy Lee Jones, Tom Cruise, and William Shatner. Race car drivers including Al Unser, Jr., Terry Labonte, Darrell Waltrip, and Jeff Gordon have also honed their skills at the Bondurant School. However, most students at the school are simply individuals with a desire to drive like professionals.

The school was started in 1968 by Bob Bondurant, who had been a very successful race car driver. He had grown up with a passion for anything on wheels and was racing motorcycles on dirt ovals by the time he was eighteen. Then he started driving sports cars, winning many races like the GT category at the prestigious Le Mans. His expertise was recognized with awards, including the Corvette Driver of the Year Award. Bob also raced Formula One cars successfully.

A very serious racing accident in 1967 forced Bob to think about the future. He decided to open a driving school and use his experience and expert knowledge of driving to teach others. The school is now located outside of Phoenix, Arizona, at the Firebird International Raceway Complex. It has a fifteen-turn, 1.6-mile race track, designed by Bob for high-performance race driving and advanced driving instruction. There is also an eight-acre pad used for advanced driver training.

An Instructor at the Bondurant School

Patrick Sallaway has a job that would delight any road warrior. As an instructor at Bondurant, he spends most of his workday behind the wheel of a full race-modified Crown Victoria Police Interceptor teaching such courses as Grand Prix Road Racing, Advanced Road Racing, High-Performance Driving, and Executive Protection/Antikidnapping. In the winter, Patrick works between 8:00 A.M. and 5:00 P.M., but in the hot summer days in Arizona, his workday begins at 6:00 A.M. and ends at 3:30 P.M.

A description of how Patrick teaches the Grand Prix Road Racing course will help you understand the work of instructors at this high-performance driving school. This particular course is designed for those who have dreamed of driving a race car or are considering a career in professional motor sports. Course graduates are eligible for an SCCA (Sports Car Club of America) Regional License as well as other competition licenses.

The first day of the course begins with the chief instructor giving the students, usually twelve, a walking tour of the facility and a description of how the course works. Then everyone goes into the classroom to learn about the basics of this type of driving, especially the physics involved in road racing, from one of the four course instructors. When this class is over, the students meet their personal instructors—one for every three drivers.

Instruction Days One and Two

Before Patrick meets the drivers who are assigned to him, he will check to make sure his personal car is both safe and clean. He will begin the lesson with a demonstration drive on the training track. Patrick describes this as a ride and a half that shows exactly what the car can do when an expert driver is at the wheel. Then he gives his drivers a demonstration of the skills they should practice first before pulling off the course. At this point, each driver gets into his or her own assigned car after safety instructions. They follow Patrick through the course as he shows them what they should be doing. Next, Patrick pulls off the course, parks, and monitors how his drivers are progressing before getting into the car of each driver to give them personal instruction. This is definitely the scariest part of being an instructor.

Through the rest of the morning session, the students will follow the same program of learning a skill from Patrick, following him on the course, and then practicing. After this three-hour driving session, there is a break for lunch and another class before the students return to the course for another three-hour driving session. The pattern for the second day is largely the same, as the drivers continue to learn and practice such fundamentals as braking, skid recognition and recovery, steering, and throttling.

Instruction Days Three and Four

On the third day of instruction, Patrick and his drivers move to the 1.6-mile road course, where he slowly introduces the track to them by showing where to brake, accelerate, and turn. He will also drive a couple of hot laps. The drivers then get into their own cars and follow Patrick through the course to learn the racing line. The rest of this day is spent in practice. Patrick rides with each driver and demonstrates what changes they need to make to improve their skills.

On the last day, the drivers will actually participate in a race. First, however, Patrick shows them how to start and obey flags. When Patrick teaches more advanced courses, he and the other instructors actually race against professional drivers. They are proud to say that they have never lost one of these races. This clearly shows you the expertise of Bondurant instructors.

Patrick's Career Path

Patrick has a burning passion for racing. By dint of hard work and saving, he started his racing career by buying a used sprint car, towing it to a track, and racing the very first night. He describes this experience as breathtaking and said it was exactly how he had imagined in his dreams. While being impossibly busy working a full-time job, repairing his own car, and racing, Patrick began to attract the attention of car owners and to drive for them.

As he kept progressing on the sprint car circuit, moving to better and better rides, he decided that he wanted to learn how to drive all types of race cars and went to a high-performance driving school. He then began racing open-wheel formula racing cars. The next step in his career was to go back to school for an advanced racing course, where he got an understanding of how driving schools operate. Patrick decided to become an instructor and applied for a job at Bondurant and was hired.

Career Satisfactions

Patrick is overwhelmingly satisfied with his career. He has a job where he is able to continue racing and at the same time spend hours each day behind the wheel of a racing car. In addition, he continues to make progress toward his ultimate goal of competing in the Indianapolis 500 race. And, along the way, he has had the opportunity to work with celebrities, active racers, and people from all over the world.

BSR, Inc.

BSR is a driver training school for accident avoidance, high performance, racing, police pursuit, security, and defensive driving. The school has three full-time instructors and several who work part-time. While the school offers a menu of courses, it should not be considered a racing school, as the focus is more on teaching security and police driver training courses. The school is based at Summit Point Raceway, seventy miles west of Washington, D.C. The 472-acre training facility has a two-mile, ten-turn racing course, giving BSR the ability to provide a challenging road on which recreational events are highlighted. Serious driver training is accomplished on real roads under the real highway situations drivers are likely to face.

What It's Like to Teach at BSR

Bruce Reichel is a full-time instructor at BSR. His introduction to this profession was definitely atypical. While working as a designer and fabricator of signs, he started painting race cars for the adjoining shop. This led to his serving as a crew member at endurance races. Bruce loved this type of racing because strategy was so important and long-term thinking was absolutely essential. When the owner of the racing team started a driving school, Bruce became an instructor. The school was originally started to teach air force pilots how to drive safely so that these highly trained individuals would not be involved in highway accidents. Then came classes for police and security personnel. Subsequent additions turned the school into one offering a wide range of courses. After Bruce started at the school, he did both amateur and professional road racing. He also has built cars and served as a crew chief. It is not unusual for instructors to work in many areas of racing.

As senior instructor at BSR, Bruce now oversees all of the other instructors and classes besides handling his teaching duties. While he primarily teaches Monday through Friday, he may also teach on the weekend. When he begins working with a student, there is a classroom session, then he demonstrates in the car what will be taught, and, finally, the student practices.

Most students think that they are good drivers; however, after driving with Bruce, they understand how good they can become. In the car, Bruce first works on establishing fundamentals, such as how to sit and how to brake. Instructors at BSR do not have to follow any established curriculum; they can use their own techniques in teaching different skills. By observation, Bruce is able to see quickly what each driver needs. His aim is to make different driving techniques natural for students. For example, when teaching skid control, he doesn't want the student to memorize the steps but rather to absorb the process so skids can be handled without thinking.

Career Advice

Bruce believes that you will not become a good driver through self-discovery. He advises those who desire to become instructors to start as students and then continue to learn through practice. He strongly believes that driving instruction is an extremely satisfactory career because it allows you to meet people from around the world and at the same time contribute to making roads a safer place for everyone.

For More Information

To learn more about becoming an instructor at a commercial driving school, contact a local driving school. Those schools that are looking for instructors often run ads in newspapers, or you can look for the names of schools in the Yellow Pages under "driving instruction." If you want to teach driver's education at a high school, try to talk to an instructor to find out what is involved in this career.

For a career as an instructor at a truck driving school, you can begin by contacting a local school or one of the schools listed in Appendix B. Career opportunities at high-performance driving schools can be investigated by calling the schools or visiting their websites.

For any career as a driving instructor, you may also be able to obtain helpful career information about safety driving courses from:

National Safety Council
1121 Spring Lake Drive
Itasca, IL 60143
www.nsc.org

CHAPTER EIGHT

More Careers Behind the Wheel

S ome people are road warriors—they enjoy each minute they are driving whether it is on a country road or an interstate. The purpose of this book is to give you ideas about careers that will let you be on the move for most of your workday. Of course, there are still more careers than have been mentioned in this book. You may have to be creative to discover them. You will find it easier if you look around while you are driving down the road for drivers who are at work behind the wheels of their vehicles. Immediately, you will observe highway patrol officers, ambulance drivers, concrete mixer drivers, and moving van drivers. Also, try browsing through an occupational handbook and consider how much driving is involved in different careers. Do the same thing while reading want ads in newspapers or visiting employment sites on the Web. Here are a few more careers that would be perfect for those who want to spend their working days on the move.

More Careers for Road Warriors

Material-Moving Operators Drive Vehicles as Big as Houses

Imagine driving a vehicle with tires that are almost twelve feet high and having to climb a ladder to enter the cab. This is the vehicle that Alysa Dutton drives every day on the job as she hauls dirt from an open-pit coal mine to a dump that actually refills previously mined areas. Her vehicle is commonly described as being about the size of a two-story house. When the bed of this giant dump truck is raised to remove dirt, it is fifty feet up in the air. Alysa is not the only woman driving such a mammoth-size truck; several other women have similar jobs at the mine. While Alysa usually drives dirt trucks, she also drives the same size coal trucks and occasionally much smaller water trucks used to keep down the dust.

In order for coal to be removed from this open-pit mine in Wyoming, layers of dirt that cover the coal must first be removed. The dirt is hauled away by six of these giant trucks so that the coal, also hauled in the same size trucks, can be taken to a hopper where it is crushed. Dirt truck drivers, like Alysa, are now driving down six benches to reach the current work area. They travel on dirt roads wide enough for two of these trucks to pass. For Alysa, the journey from the spot where a huge shovel places three buckets (240 tons) of dirt in her dump truck to where she dumps it is a distance of one to two miles. She will make this trip about seventy times in a day. This is certainly a job for those who want to be on the move, as Alysa only stops driving for seventy seconds to have the truck loaded and again when the dirt is dumped, except for breaks.

You don't need a license or special classes to drive one of these giant trucks. The only classes that Alysa attended were safety and hazard training. She learned to drive by riding in the cab with an experienced driver and then driving with her mentor driver in the cab until she was ready to solo.

Career Satisfaction

The cab of Alysa's giant dump truck is designed to make her job pleasant. Her seat has springs so she has a comfortable ride over the dirt roads, and she has a radio and cassette player as well as air-conditioning. Because the mine operates 365 days a year, twenty-four hours a day, Alysa works twelve-hour shifts rotating between day and night. She will work four days, have seven off, then four nights followed by three off, then three days followed by one off, and finally three nights and three off before starting the same work schedule all over again. While Alysa finds it difficult at times to switch from working days to nights, she really likes having seven days off at a stretch, which can be extended to fourteen if she takes a week's vacation.

The downside to this job is the monotony involved in doing the same thing over and over at as fast a pace as possible. However, Alysa has learned how to best use her seventy seconds of free time when the truck is being loaded. She has managed to read lots of books in these short segments of time and exercise with the dumbbells she carries with her in the cab. When she has to wait for the truck in front of her to unload, she uses the truck's ladder as her own stair-step exerciser. Alysa firmly believes that you must be an individual who can entertain yourself in order to enjoy this job, which offers excellent pay and benefits.

Sales Representatives Spend Considerable Time on the Road

Bill Haas is a sales representative for an engineering firm that sells sensors to car and automotive accessories manufacturers to use in their plants. While Bill's job is a sales job, it is also one that necessarily involves considerable time on the road, as he visits plants throughout the state of Indiana to make calls on engineers and maintenance people. In a typical year, he will travel between twenty-five thousand to thirty thousand miles and be able to spend most nights at home.

Few people realize how many car and automotive accessories plants there are in Indiana. Bill regularly makes sales calls on twenty plants and will visit some every other week. His day may begin as early as 5:30 A.M., when he leaves home to call on a nearby plant by 6:00 A.M. Once he gets to a plant, his visit may last from forty-five minutes to a half a day or more. Some plants are so large that it takes him considerable time to even find the right people to talk to about his company's products. When Bill visits plants close to his home, he obviously will not spend as much time on the road. However, there are many days in which half of his workday is spent on the road. As he drives from plant to plant, Bill enjoys listening to sports on the radio. However, his road time is also business time, as he talks on his cell phone to the office and makes appointments for plant visits.

The Car as an Office

Sales representatives have to show their products to prospective buyers, so Bill carries samples in the car. When he leaves the car to visit a plant, he loads a case with items from the stock of supplies filling the trunk and backseat of his car. There is a milk carton of catalogs and another with literature about products that will be in the next catalog. There are boxes of all kinds of giveaways, including hats, pens, pencils, and pocketknives, for the people he visits in the plants to keep his product visible to them. Within the car, Bill also has such office equipment as a Palm Pilot, planner, hands-free cell phone, and pager. His car is truly equipped so that it is a minioffice for him.

Career Advice

If you choose a career as a sales representative, Bill wants you to realize that this is not a structured job. You will make your own schedule. It will up to you to decide what time you will start to work and how many calls to make in a day. There is also the possibility of working long hours to get a half day free. And, of course, if you have a job like Bill's, you must enjoy working on the road instead of in an office. He only spends one day a week in the office. This is Bill's first job, and he thinks it is an excellent one because it lets him see what role so many people play in the manufacture of cars and automotive accessories.

Marketing Service Representatives Travel

Far more occupations than you probably ever imagined require employees to spend more than half of their time in travel. Nevertheless, these occupations exist in almost every industry. Dustin Crandall, a marketing service representative for a large heavy-equipment manufacturer, has one of these jobs. He spends half of his work time in a car traveling to dealerships in Connecticut, New York, and New Jersey for his company. Dustin's job is to make sure that the dealers are able to correct any defects in material and workmanship or failures that a machine may have. He represents the company and acts as a liaison in communications between the dealerships and company headquarters.

Since Dustin divides his time between five dealerships, he must travel two or three days a week. Depending on the distance, he often stays overnight in a hotel. With this type of travel schedule, Dustin is only in his office one or two days a week. Therefore, he always takes a laptop and cell phone with him so that he can work while on the road and at night in hotels. Most of the work that Dustin does at night involves downloading E-mails and checking his phone messages. There have been some occasions that Dustin has been out of the office for entire weeks on the road. He tries to schedule his trips so that he can be in the office at least one day a week. This gives him the opportunity to get caught up on outstanding issues, report any new problems, and answer questions through E-mail and on the phone.

A Car Is a Job Perk

Since most of Dustin's travels are by car, the company provides him with a company car. They also pay for all his expenses while traveling as well as all expenses associated with the car, including the cost of gas, oil changes, tolls, maintenance and repairs, and even car washes. The only charges that Dustin incurs on the car are when he uses it for his own personal use. Then the company charges him a small fee for each mile he drives. This road warrior likes the advantages of having a career that not only lets him have a company car, but also lets him determine his own traveling schedule. For someone to choose a career like Dustin's, they should like traveling, solving problems with products, and negotiating with others.

Meter Readers Are Drivers

On the job as a meter reader, Ross Bellow drives as much as twenty thousand miles in a year. He isn't always driving in his car from meter to meter, as he walks some of his twenty-one routes. Also, on some of his routes, he will drive to a certain point and then walk a circle before returning to his car. Nevertheless, this is a job that involves a lot of driving. Ross's driving routes will vary from twenty to forty-five miles in length.

At each stop, Ross will read the meter in seconds and enter the information in a handheld computer. What takes the most time in this job is accessing the meters on some of the routes. They can be under manhole covers, in backyards, and even on roofs. Plus, there is always the ever-present danger of running into unfriendly dogs and the discomfort of working in bad weather.

On a typical day, Ross will arrive at the utility office at 6:30 A.M. and then drive to the start of his route. He is expected to read all the meters on his route, which he always does. By 3:00 P.M., he is usually able to be back at the utility office to turn in the computer. As a meter reader, he is paid by the hour, uses his own car, and receives a car allowance.

While this is a good job for individuals who want driving to play an important role in their workdays, it is also one that is headed toward extinction. When the technology is perfected,

meters will be read remotely by computers that have been sent
the data over phone lines.

Police Officers Log Many Hours
in Their Patrol Cars

Choose to become a police officer who patrols for a city, county,
or state, and you have chosen a job that will put you on the move
throughout your shift. Bryan Musgrove, a county patrol officer,
actually spends more than 90 percent of his time on the job in a
car. At the start of a shift, he reports to his assigned station for
roll call and to be updated on new regulations and any outstanding crimes from the prior shifts, as well as suspects and vehicles
to look for throughout the shift. Bryan then gets in his patrol car
and begins traveling around his assigned zone.

Traveling by himself in his vehicle, Bryan will answer any 911
calls in his zone, enforce traffic laws, and patrol neighborhoods.
He is never sure what will happen out on the road on his shift.
Throughout the day, he will keep a record of his activities, to be
turned in at the end of his shift when he returns to the station
for debriefing. During Bryan's six-days-on and three-days-off
schedule, he will work two different zones in the county. While
Bryan finds his career extremely fulfilling because of the positive
impact that his job has on the community, he is not enthusiastic
about the shift hours that he must work at times.

Career Advice

Bryan recommends taking classes in law and criminal justice to
see if you will enjoy a career in law enforcement. He also advises
young people considering a career like his to take part in a Police
Explorer Program as an introduction to police work. And to get
a picture of what it would be like to be a patrol officer, he sug-
gests doing a ride along with a local police officer in order to see
firsthand exactly what is involved in this career.

Security Guards Drive on Patrol

Security guards can work in one location or be assigned to mobile patrol work. Road warriors will, of course, be interested in those jobs in which security guards drive from location to location and conduct security checks. Typically, patrol guards are assigned to either a residential or a commercial area, such as a shopping center or business park. Most wear uniforms provided by the security company and may or may not carry a weapon. They usually drive company cars marked with the name of the security company that employs them. These cars may have yellow patrol lights and a spotlight. In order to communicate with the company dispatcher, police, fire department, and wreckers, they use cell phones or radios.

On the Job

Patrol guards need to be very observant. In residential areas, they are looking for unfamiliar cars, criminal activity, and residents with problems. While residential guards will most often drive through assigned neighborhoods at night, guards working in business areas typically are employed on a twenty-four-hour basis. Not only do these guards watch for criminal activity, they also are concerned with such things as traffic and the functioning of stoplights and lawn sprinklers. In both residential and business areas, the guards respond to emergency calls. Throughout the course of their work, security patrol guards check in electronically along their routes at specific locations. This lets the security company know where they are and ensures their safety. Another task of the guards is to write comprehensive reports of any incidents that occur on their shifts.

Armored Car Guards Stay on the Move

Armored cars are very distinctive and easily recognizable vehicles. You have probably seen them on the road as well as stopped to make deliveries and pickups. The driver of the car as well as the accompanying guard or guards are on the move most of the day, so this is truly a job for road warriors. At the same time, this job can be extremely hazardous. When guards are out of the armored car and transporting money and other valuables to and from banks and businesses, a number of them have been robbed and shot in recent years, so armored car guards usually wear bullet-proof vests.

Realtors Drive on the Job

Marge Blake-Myers is a very successful realtor who is always one of the top ten salespeople in a company of 125 agents selling residential properties in Northern California. Because Marge doesn't just list and sell properties in one community, she spends a great deal of time in her car. She may even spend an entire day showing homes to just one client. Plus, most clients want to visit prospective homes more than once before they put in a bid. Additional time is spent in her car every Thursday between 9:30 A.M. and 2:30 P.M., when Marge drives to open houses showcasing all the new houses that have come on the market that week. Not only does Marge show homes to buyers, she also visits the homes of clients who want to sell their homes.

While realtors, like Marge, spend considerable time on the move in their cars, her career is really centered on selling homes. Much of her time is spent in the office doing all the paperwork and negotiations involved in the listing, buying, and selling of properties.

If you want a career as a realtor, the first step is to obtain a license. Most states will require you to complete between thirty and ninety hours of classroom instruction before taking the licensing test, which includes questions on basic real estate transactions and laws affecting the sale of properties. Once you have a license, you may either work for yourself, as two-thirds of all realtors do, or work for a real estate firm. This is one job in which you are at the beck and call of your clients. Expect to work nights and on weekends and more than fifty-hour weeks in order to be a successful realtor.

The demand for realtors is very sensitive to swings in the economy. During periods of declining economic activity and tight credit, the volume of sales and the resulting demand for realtors falls. Nevertheless, this is a career in which the highest 10 percent of realtors earn more than $83,000 a year.

Drag Racers Are Speedy Drivers

Tony Schumacher's profession is drag racing. While he has had other jobs to supplement his income, racing has always been his career. Driving is definitely in Tony's blood, as his father was a drag racer, and he can't remember when he wasn't going to tracks. As soon as the local drag strip opened in the spring after his sixteenth birthday, he was there driving a 1986 Trans Am. Then for the next two years after completing high school, Tony raced a 1969 Chevelle that his dad and two friends worked on with him. At this time, he had no idea what his future in racing would be. He did know that he was having fun and going very fast for an eighteen-year-old, doing a quarter mile in ten seconds.

At nineteen, Tony went to the Skip Barber Racing School and learned to drive Formula Fords. After road racing for one year, he had to choose which way his racing career would go: road racing or drag racing. Tony opted for drag racing and started driving a Super-Comp Dragster in competition while attending college. Next, he was asked to drive an Odyssey Jet Dragster, an exhibition car, which he did for two years. Then, he decided that he wanted to return to competition and bought an Alcohol Funny Car that he and his friends constantly worked on to maximize its speed. A blower explosion totaled this car, and Tony was hired by the Peake brothers to drive a dragster in the fastest class. His success was immediate—he finished second in his first race.

In 1999, Tony's father obtained a new sponsorship for him. Since then, he has won the Winston Championship and finished number two in points in 2000. Tony has become a top drag racer in the United States and no longer needs to work at any job but racing.

While races only take a few seconds, the rest of his time is devoted to testing the car and working with the mechanics to make it go even faster. They have been quite successful. Tony was the first driver to ever run 330.23 miles per hour in 1999. Tony is in his early thirties and plans to continue this career into his fifties.

Career Advice

If you want to be a drag racer, Tony feels it is imperative to surround yourself with the right people and to pay attention to their advice. He also points out that you should not race on streets, which is not only dangerous but doesn't teach you how to race. Tony advises you to go to the track where race people will help you get started in this career.

A Career in Racing—from Stock Cars to the Indianapolis 500

So many race car drivers have similar backgrounds. Like Tony, Steve Chassey's father had been involved in racing. And he fondly remembers summer vacations driving across the country and stopping along the way to see races. With this background, Steve knew from an early age that he wanted to be a race car driver. He began to fulfill his dream at age seventeen by racing a stock car, which he had built, on quarter-mile paved tracks. In his very first race, he qualified high enough to make the feature race. Steve went to college but did not stay long because his racing career was taking off.

At the start of his career, Steve always worked other jobs. A stint in Vietnam, however, interrupted his career before it really started. When he returned, he began racing sprint cars and also midget cars.

At this time, he was working in his own auto repair body shop during the day and on his car at night and racing throughout California on the weekend. Steve met with considerable success in sprint car racing and was named Rookie of the Year in California.

From California, Steve moved to the Midwest with the car that his father had purchased for him before Vietnam. Although he had done well with the car in California, it did not have the quality of other cars in the Midwest, where racing was more professional. He began to work for Gary Bettenhausen, a well-known Indianapolis 500 racer, building race cars while at the same time driving sprint and championship dirt cars. By now, he had done well enough in racing that he was receiving offers to drive cars and was able to ask owners for a ride. Steve was paid for racing in the same way as other drivers. The owners gave him 40 percent of what a car earned in a race or 50 percent if he won the race.

The Indianapolis 500

After several years, Steve was able to support himself through racing and doing TV commentary on racing. Besides racing sprint and championship dirt cars, he began to race Indy cars. It is not easy to qualify for the Indianapolis 500. First, Steve had to practice in Indy cars and race at other tracks before he even attempted to enter the 500, which has been called "the greatest spectacle in racing." He was not too successful initially because his car was substandard. However, with a lot of practice and hints from other drivers, he began to meet with success and was able to take even subpar cars to top-ten finishes. As his driving skills increased, he was able to qualify three times for the Indianapolis 500 and to finish eleventh in one of the races.

Few racers have long careers. As Steve became older, his reflexes slowed and his desire to race decreased, so he decided it was time to retire. He did not abandon racing entirely. He has since started working in the business of insuring cars, racetracks, and drivers.

Career Advice

Steve advises anyone who wants to drive race cars to follow his or her dream. He believes that the best way to get started is with go-carts and then to move up through more demanding cars and tracks. However, because so many do not get to the top echelon as he did, Steve believes that you need to get a good education in case you are unable to fully realize your dreams. He does regret not completing college, as it would have increased his career options after his racing career was over.

Animal Control Officers Drive Vans and Trucks

If you choose to be an animal control officer as Linda Adams did, you can expect to be on the move 80 percent of the time in a van or truck. Before you get this job, however, you will have to demonstrate that you have a knowledge of animals; a law enforcement background that includes course work in arrest, search, seizure, and citation authority; firearms training; and the ability to drive a big truck. Linda gained these skills through college classes and a previous job as a ranger.

Linda worked for one of the largest counties in California and would easily drive 150 miles in a day as she made from twenty to thirty stops handling the following responsibilities:

- Patrolling county cities for stray animals
- Responding to animal emergencies such as removing animals from hot cars, horses from canals, and rattlesnakes from freeway rest stops
- Answering animal complaint calls (barking dogs)
- Taking care of dog bites
- Investigating animal welfare and cruelty
- Picking up food donations for animal shelters

On the Job

Linda's schedule as an animal control officer was not an easy one. She worked four ten-hour days and every weekend, as well as being on call two nights a week. Typically, her day would begin at 7:00 A.M., when she and her fellow officers arrived at the shelter and found out what needed to be done immediately. During the day, additional calls would constantly come in for emergencies as well as other animal control problems. By 7:30 A.M., Linda, wearing a law enforcement uniform, a badge, and a name tag, was ready to climb behind the wheel of the one-ton truck that she drove.

During the course of her workday, she would return to the shelter with stray dogs and cats and to the wildlife rescue center with wild animals whenever the cages on her truck were full. This would usually necessitate at least two trips a day. Because stops to handle problems were often quite far apart in the county, this was truly a job for someone who liked to drive. However, there are risks involved with this job in which you frequently subdue and capture animals and have to deal with very angry people. However, the independence of being out on the road by yourself is a great plus for most road warriors.

Movers Stay on the Move

Carl Freeman is a mover who works as an independent contractor for a large international moving company. He owns his own tractor, and the company furnishes the trailer and assigns him to moving jobs. Carl hires helpers to assist him in loading and unloading the trailer. So besides being a road warrior, Carl also functions as a businessperson.

To keep Carl busy and on the move, the company dispatcher tries to schedule several loading jobs within a central area to fill the trailer. In a typical workweek, Carl may spend the first three days getting the trailer loaded, followed by a few days of driving. Then, he will work through the weekend to unload everything before starting the cycle all over again. During a given day, Carl can work up to fifteen hours: ten hours of driving and five hours of physical labor. All of his time must be logged and sent back to the company every day.

The Loading Process

Before Carl begins to load the trailer, he must obtain helpers. Upon arriving at a home, Carl greets the home owners and introduces himself. He then asks for a tour of the house and explains the loading procedure. While the local helpers begin moving prepackaged boxes outside and lining them up on the driveway, Carl goes through the entire house, inventorying the items to be shipped and labeling them with stickers. He also records the condition of each piece carefully, noting any damage. Next, he wraps all the furniture with packing blankets and tape, ensuring that they are well padded for the long ride ahead. Then, Carl works with the helpers to disassemble such bulky items as kitchen tables, pool tables, and headboards that could not be securely packed.

Once all Carl's work in the house is complete, he begins to load the trailer because he is solely responsible for its contents. In the loading process, he touches every box and piece of furniture in the entire house. Once everything is loaded, Carl completes all the paperwork and reviews it with the home owners. If he has a full load, he begins driving; otherwise, he makes other stops to fill the trailer before taking off.

On the Road and Unloading

Due to the hours that Carl works and the vast distances between locations, he spends about 85 percent of his time away from home. While on the road, he sleeps in his extended cab semi-truck. It is fully loaded with a microwave, refrigerator, and an air-conditioning unit. Once Carl reaches his destination, he contacts the shippers to verify the unloading date and time. He also hires helpers to assist him in the unloading. At the home, Carl again requests a tour to find out where certain items will go. Unloading then begins. The home owners have a sheet with all the label numbers listed, and they mark off each number when the box or item is unloaded. Once the trailer is unloaded, Carl and his helpers reassemble items and remove packing materials from the home. The job is complete when he goes through the paperwork with the home owners.

Skills Required for Movers

It is not enough for movers to be road warriors with expert driving skills. They must also have solid people skills that allow them to establish quickly a solid, working relationship with home owners and helpers. Since there is a great deal of paperwork that must be filled out and filed, movers need to be organized. Plus, with all the lifting and moving of heavy items, they must be strong physically. Finally, in order to be successful as an independent contractor in the moving industry, you must be willing to work very hard.

Overview of Job Opportunities

The future is bright for people who want to be on the move and other road warriors. Businesses will always need truckers to haul goods to keep the economy humming. And all people must rely on buses, taxis, vans, and limousines to meet some of their transportation needs. Plus, almost everyone who wishes to drive a vehicle, whether it is a car, truck, bus, or race car, needs some help in mastering the intricacies of driving. In fact, such training is often required by law. The next time you are on the road, look at all the other drivers and observe how many have found careers on the move. Today, road warriors are fortunate to have a choice of so many different and exciting careers behind the wheel.

Checklist for Quality Truck Driver Training Programs

F ormal training is the most reliable way to learn the many special skills required for safe truck driving. The more skills that are learned in supervised training, the fewer that need to be learned on the job. Such training is available from private schools, public education institutions, and in-house motor carrier training programs. Because of the important role in truck safety, the trucking industry has implemented minimum standards by which to measure training programs. The standards are administered through the Professional Truck Driver Institute (PTDI). You can contact PTDI by writing to:

Professional Truck Driver Institute
2200 Mill Road
Alexandria, VA 22314

Because training institutions voluntarily certify their courses to meet PTDI standards, not all schools have chosen to certify their courses. You can use the following checklist to evaluate a tractor-trailer driver training course against PTDI standards if it is not certified. All PTDI-certified courses meet these standards. The checklist is only a brief treatment of the standards by which truck driver training quality is measured. It is not intended to provide an exhaustive evaluation of standards. This checklist is reprinted with permission of the Professional Truck Driver Institute.

Course Administration

Truth in Advertising

- Is the course accurately and clearly defined and explained in printed materials on topics such as costs, training provided, outcomes, classroom hours, and actual individual driving time?

- Does the school actually provide the course claimed?

- Can the school meet its obligations to students, employees, and employers?

Chain of Command

- Is the organizational framework clearly defined, showing responsibility for instruction and administration?

Administrative Institutional Support

- Does administration provide appropriate facilities and up-to-date equipment and training materials?

Course Goals

- Are there clearly stated goals that match the needs of students and the trucking industry?

Administrative Qualifications

- Is the course planned and directed by persons experienced in training tractor-trailer drivers?

- Are administrative staff qualified for their assignments?

Student Eligibility

- Are there clear, written eligibility requirements that are followed?

- Must an applicant meet minimum Department of Transportation (DOT), state, federal, and/or local laws and regulations related to drug screens, age, physical condition, licensing, driving ability, and driving record as stated in the school's admissions policy?

Written Policies

- Are there written policies regarding safety, liability, and rules?

Recruitment and Admissions

- Do admissions follow written procedures?

- Are enrollment agreements required?

Curriculum

Course Outline

- Does the course outline clearly identify units of instruction including their sequence, broad purpose, and general content?

- Is the course outline provided to all participants and others?

Course Content and Objectives

- Is the course composed of units of instruction that cover the knowledge and skills required to operate a tractor-trailer safely and properly?

Print Materials

- Are instructional materials appropriate for the ability of the trainee?

- Are materials provided to each trainee?

- Do the materials contain up-to-date information?

Audiovisual/Multimedia Materials

- Are materials up-to-date, accurate, and fit into the lessons?

Instructional Personnel

Instructor Qualifications

Instructors should possess a combination of education and experiences that clearly qualify them for their assignments. At least the following elements are included:

- Do instructors have at least three years of experience as licensed, successful tractor-trailer drivers with a good driving record?

- Do instructors meet state requirements and school policy?

- Do instructors meet Part 391 of the Federal Motor Carrier Safety Regulations?

- Do instructors have a high school diploma or its equivalent?

- Do instructors have teacher/instructional skills?

- Do instructors have a state license or permit, if required?

Instructor Staff Development and Supervision

- Are instructors thoroughly trained in the curriculum?

- Do instructors participate in a regular staff development program?

- Are instructors carefully supervised and evaluated?

Training Vehicles

Condition of Vehicles

- Are vehicles in good mechanical condition?

- Do they meet safety requirements, contain occupant-restraint systems for all occupants, and contain working emergency equipment?

Industry Standard for Vehicles

- Are training vehicles comparable in size and power to those used by motor carriers in the area?

Instruction

Curriculum Content

- Does instruction cover the subject areas identified by PTDI curriculum and skill standards? (See PTDI's "Primary Functions/Duties of a Tractor-Trailer Driver")

- Does classroom instruction include the use of aids such as films, displays, textbooks, models, charts, and so on?

Instructional Time

- Does *each* student receive at least 104 (sixty-minute) hours in classroom and lab time? (Lab includes time on the range under the supervision of an instructor. Observation time does not count as instructional time.)

- Does *each* student receive at least forty-four (sixty-minute) hours of actual behind-the-wheel (BTW) time? (This is time with hands actually on the wheel, with at least twelve hours on the range and twelve on the road and the other twenty hours on either.)

Classroom Conditions

- Is the learning environment safe, sanitary, and comfortable?

- Are furnishings, light, temperature, ventilation, and space adequate?

Student/Instructor/Truck Ratio

- Does classroom and lab instruction average one instructor for not more than each group of thirty students during the year and never exceed thirty-six students?

- Is there never more than one instructor to three trucks on the range?

- During driving, is there one instructor per truck and never more than four trainees in the truck?

Lesson Plans

- Do instructors use lesson plans to guide each session?

- Are students provided with behind-the-wheel lesson driving procedures along with a list of safety rules for street driving?

Range Conditions

- Is the range safe and protected from the hazards from other road users?

- Is the range free of obstructions, and does the surface enable the driver to maneuver without loss of control?

Street Instruction

- Is driving practiced under various roadway and traffic conditions?

- Is the trailer loaded with a minimum of fifteen thousand pounds during at least 25 percent of street instruction time?

- Are night driving principles taught and practiced?

Independent Study

- Independent study may be substituted for classroom instruction for up to one-third of the classroom instruction if it is sufficiently documented and quality materials are used.

Tests

- Do written classroom/lab exams test mastery of a sample of knowledge objectives for each unit of instruction?

- Do range tests assess student proficiency in (a) fundamental vehicle control skills and (b) routine driving procedures?

- Do road or on-the-street tests assess the objectives of the training?

- Do road tests use routes that permit a broad range of observations, and are they planned in advance?

- Are BTW proficiency tests administered with a standard van or box-type tandem axle trailer with a minimum length of forty-five feet and with a tractor with a tandem axle?

Graduation

- Does a student have to successfully complete the course equivalent to PTDI content and hours, including tests and road tests before graduation?

- Does a student secure a CDL before graduation is conferred?

Outcomes

Follow-up

- Is a follow-up system used to determine student employment verification and to provide feedback on the effectiveness of the training?

- Does follow-up provide information on why graduates are not employed?

- Are student critiques of the school used?

In-Training Data

- Is an in-training file maintained for each trainee?

- Does the file contain training records, attendance/time records, test results, unit completion, and progress information?

Permanent Records

- Are records of graduates kept for at least ten years and securely maintained?

- Are transcripts provided upon request?

Behind-the-Wheel Time Records

- Does each student keep a "driver duty status record" to document time behind the wheel?

- Are both the student and instructor required to sign off on the record?

Externship Option

An externship option allows a training course to defer up to fourteen hours of the required forty-four behind-the-wheel hours to a trucking firm. For each three hours driven with a trucking company, one hour of behind-the-wheel time may be earned for credit. If a school uses this option, a number of conditions must be met:

- Is there weekly student evaluation?

- Are there objectives that specify and direct training?

- Are skilled and experienced driver-trainers teaching and monitoring training?

- Are quality training materials used?

- Does the curriculum describe the elements of training that the trainee will experience?

- Is there performance assessment of critical skills?

- Is there a system of feedback and record keeping for the trainee, both for the trainee and the school?

- Are program policies on issues such as attendance, pay, insurance, and liability clearly articulated?

- Is there a formal agreement between the carrier and the training institution?

To find the answers to these questions, you may question school personnel, current students or graduates, and motor carriers who hire graduates from the school.

For more information about PTDI standards, industry news, or job opportunities, or to request a booklet on careers in trucking, visit the website at www.ptdi.org.

Schools for Entry-Level Truck Driver Training

The following schools offer entry-level truck driver training courses that are certified to meet the standards of the Professional Truck Driver Institute (PTDI). The list is believed to be accurate as of the date compiled. However, it is the responsibility of users and prospective students to determine whether a specific course is certified before enrolling in a driver training course. Many schools have a number of truck driving courses. Please note that only the course number(s) shown below are certified by PTDI. The status of any school's course may be determined by checking the website at www.ptdi.org.

PTDI-certified courses are currently offered at seventy-three schools in thirty states and in Canada. Generally, these courses are certified in early April, August, and December. Check after the third week of these months for updates. This list is reprinted with the permission of Professional Truck Driver Institute, Inc.

ALASKA
Center for Employment Education
1049 Whitney Road
Anchorage, AK 99501
www.cee-ak.com
Course Name: Basic Truck Driver
Course No.: 92005-01-01

ARIZONA
American Institute of Technology (AIT)
440 South Fifty-fourth Avenue
Phoenix, AZ 85043
www.ait-schools.com
Course Name: Professional Truck Driver
Course No.: 98002-01-01

M.S. Carriers Professional Driving Academy - Phoenix
6021 West Sherman Street
Phoenix, AZ 85043
www.mscarriers.com
Course Name: M. S. Carriers Professional Driving Academy
Course No.: 99021-01-01

Swift Transportation
2200 South Seventy-fifth Avenue
Phoenix, AZ 85043
www.swiftrans. com
Course Name: Swift Tractor Trailer Driving Program
Course No.: 98009-01-01

ARKANSAS
Arkansas Commercial Driver Training Institute
Arkansas State University-Newport
7648 Victory Boulevard
Newport, AR 72112
www.asun.arknet.edu
Course Name: DTI 11005 Commercial Driver Training
Course No.: 00013-01-01

CALIFORNIA
Western Pacific Truck School
4565 North Golden State Boulevard
Fresno, CA 93722
www.wptruckschool.com
Course Name: Advanced Tractor Trailer Operator
    Program—180 Hours
Course No.: 98015-03-02

Western Pacific Truck School
2316 Nickerson Drive
Modesto, CA 95358
www.wptruckschool.com
Course Name: Advanced Tractor Trailer Operator
    Program—180 hours
Course No.: 98015-02-02

Western Pacific Truck School
1002 North Broadway
Stockton, CA 95207
www.wptruckschool.com
Course Name: Advanced Tractor Trailer Operator
    Program—180 hours
Course No.: 98015-01-02

DELAWARE
Delaware Technical & Community College
PO Box 610, Route 18
Georgetown, DE 19947
www.dtcc.edu/owens/truck
Course Name: Commercial Transportation Certificate Program
Course No.: 00003-01-01

IDAHO
Sage Technical Services
207 South Thirty-fourth Avenue
Caldwell, ID 83605
www.sageschools.com
Course Name: TTD 150—Tractor Trailer Driver, Basic
Course No.: 00014-01-01

ILLINOIS
John Wood Community College
Transportation Program
150 South Forty-eighth Street
Quincy, IL 62301
www.jwcc.edu/instruct/truck
Course Name: Truck Driver Training
Course No.: 94003-00-01

INDIANA
CDL Plus (North American Van Lines)
5001 U.S. Highway 30 West
Fort Wayne, IN 46818
www.cdlplus.com
Course Name: RSD Inexperienced Owner/Operator Program
Course No.: 99019-01-01

Vincennes University Tractor-Trailer Driver Training
2175 South Hoffman Road
Indianapolis, IN 46241
www.vinu.edu/atc
Course Name: Eight-Week Tractor-Trailer Driver Training
   Program
Course No.: 00014-01-01

Iowa
Des Moines Area Community College
2081 Northeast Fifty-fourth Avenue
Des Moines, IA 50313
www.dmacc.org
Course Name: Commercial Vehicle Operator Program
Course No.: 91002-00-01

Kirkwood Community College
6301 Kirkwood Boulevard SW
P.O. Box 2068
Cedar Rapids, IA 52406
www.kirkwood.cc.ia.us
Course Name: Four-Week Truck Driving Program
Course No.: 99018-01-01

Ruan Transportation
666 Grand Avenue
Des Moines, IA 50309
Course Name: Ruan Transportation Management Systems
Course No.: 98019-01-01

Kentucky
Super Service Truck Driver Training
P.O. Box 3070
Somerset, KY 42564
www.supser.com
Course Name: Truck Driver Training
Course No.: 00012-01-01

LOUISIANA
TransportSafe Training Center
13801 Old Gentilly Road
New Orleans, LA 70189
Course Name: Professional Truck Driver Program
Course No.: 00010-01-01

MAINE
ProDrive of Maine
136 U.S. Route One
Scarborough, ME 04074
P.O. Box 4101
Portland, ME 04101
www.prodrivemaine.com
Course Name: Class A Driving
Course No.: 99022-01-01

MARYLAND
All-State Career
2200 Broening Highway, Suite 160
Baltimore, MD 21224
Course Name: Advanced Tractor Trailer Driver Program
Course No.: 99012-02-01

Professional Truck Driver Program
Frederick Community College
8042B Reichs Ford Road
Frederick, MD 21704
www.fcc.cc.md.us/continuing_education
Course Name: Professional Truck Driver Program
Course No.: 99005-01-01

MICHIGAN
Baker College of Flint
100 North Delaney
Owosso, MI 48867
http://trucking.baker.edu
Course Name: Truck Driving Certificate
Course No.: 99015-01-01

International Truck Driving School, Inc.
5700 Nelson A. Miles Parkway
Grayling, MI 49738
Course Name: Basic Truck Driver 206
Course No.: 88001-05-01

MISSOURI
South Central Career Center
1009 Jackson Street
West Plains, MO 65775
Course Name: Tractor Trailer Driver Training
Course No.: 00008-01-0

Southern Missouri Truck Driving School
105 Arnold Boulevard
Malden, MO 63863
Course Name: Tractor Trailer Driving (No Experience)
Course No.: 99017-01-01

MONTANA
SAGE Technical Services
3044 Hesper Road
Billings, MT 59102
www.sageschools.com
Course Name: TTD 150
Course No.: 91003-01-01; 91003-01-02

NEBRASKA
Northeast Community College
801 East Benjamin Avenue
P.O. Box 469
Norfolk, NE 68702
Course Name: Professional Truck Driver Training
Course No.: 95003-00-01

NEW JERSEY
Smith & Solomon School of Tractor Trailer Driving
721 Cuthbert Boulevard
Cherry Hill, NJ 08002
www.smithsolomon.com
Course Name: Tractor Trailer (CDL/A) Driver Program
Course No.: 00002-02-01

Smith & Solomon School of Tractor Trailer Driving
45 Kilmer Road
Edison, NJ 08817
www.smithsolomon.com
Course Name: Tractor Trailer (CDL/A) Driver Program
Course No.: 00002-03-01

NEW MEXICO
Albuquerque Tech/Voc Institute
525 Buena Vista SE
Albuquerque, NM 87106
www.tvi.cc.nm.us
Course Name: Truck Driving—Day Course
Course No.: 90001-00-01

Mesa Technical College
Commercial Truck Driving Program
911 South Tenth Street
Tucumcari, NM 88401
Course Name: Truck Driving
Course No.: 98021-01-01

NEW YORK
Commercial Driver Training
600 Patton Avenue
West Babylon, NY 11704
www.ctdschool.com
Course Name: Career Training I
Course No.: 89010-00-01

National Tractor Trailer School, Inc.
175 Katherine Street
Buffalo, NY 14210
www.ntts-inc.com
Course Name: Commercial Driver's Course
Course No.: 98001-02-01
Course Name: Commercial Driver's Course Externship
Course No.: 98001-02-04

National Tractor Trailer School, Inc.
4650 Buckley Road
Liverpool, NY 13088
www.ntts-inc.com
Course Name: Commercial Driver's Course
Course No.: 98001-01-01
Course Name: Commercial Driver's Course Externship Program
Course No.: 98001-01-04
Course Name: Contract Training Course
Course No.: 98001-01-05

NORTH CAROLINA
Future Truckers of America
1095A West Dixie Drive
Asheboro, NC 27203
www.futuretruckers.com
Course Name: Professional Driver Training
Course No.: 99014-01-01

Isothermal Community College/SAGE Technical Services
P.O. Box 804
Spindale, NC 28160
www.isothermal.cc.nc.us
Course Name: Professional Truck Driver Training
Course No.: 00005-01-01

OHIO
Mid-Ohio Valley Truck Driver Training
Route 2
Marietta, OH 45750
www.washingtoncocareerctr.com
Course Name: Five-Week, 200-Hour Course
Course No.: 00009-01-01

U.S. Xpress Enterprises, Inc.
P.O. Box 70
Medway, OH 45341
www.usxpress.com
Course Name: U.S. Xpress Professional Driver Training Course
Course No.: 98003-01-01

OKLAHOMA
Ardmore Truck Driving School/ATDS
P.O. Box 40
Gene Autry, OK 73436
Course Name: PTD—100
Course No.: 88001-04-01

Central Tech Transportation & Safety Education
3 CT Circle
Drumright, OK 74030
www.tdt-ok.com
Course Name: Central Tech Truck Driver Training
Course No.: 99013-01-01

OREGON
Rogue Community College
8495 Crater Lake Highway, Building 240
White City, OR 97503
www.rogue.cc.or.us/truck/home.htm
Course Name: Commercial Truck Driving
Course No.: 99023-01-01

Western Pacific Truck School of Oregon
8145 Southeast Eighty-second Avenue
Portland, OR 97266
www.wptruckschool.com
Course Name: Advanced Tractor Trailer Operator
    Program—180 hours
Course No.: 98015-06-02

PENNSYLVANIA
All State Career
501 Seminole
Lester, PA 19029
Course Name: Advanced Tractor Trailer Driver Program
Course No.: 98004-01-01; 98004-01-02; 98004-01-03;
    98004-01-04

Clearfield County Career & Technology Center
Rural Route 1, Box 5
Clearfield, PA 16830
www.ccctc.org
Course Name: Truck Driver Training
Course No.: 00007-01-01

Lebanon County Career School
18 East Weidman Street
Lebanon, PA 17046
Course Name: TTD—150
Course No.: 96003-00-01

Lehigh Career & Technical Institute (in partnership with
    SAGE Technical Services)
4500 Education Park Drive
Schnecksville, PA 18078
www.lcti.org
Course Name: Professional Tractor Trailer Driving Program
Course No.: 93003-00-01

Pittsburgh Institute of Aeronautics (PIA)
Truck Driving Program
P.O. Box 18078
Pittsburgh, PA 15236
www.truckers.org
Course Name: Full-Time, 200 Hours
Course No.: 98010-01-01

PIA Truck Driving Program of Indiana County
Indiana Learning Center
200 Babcock Drive
Homer City, PA 15748
www.truckers.org
Course Name: Full-Time, 200 Hours
Course No.: 00017-01-01

Professional Drivers Academy
P.O. Box 475
Housels Run Road
Milton Industrial Park
Milton, PA 17847

Course Name: Six Weeks, 240 Hours
Course No.: 98013-01-01
Course Name: Twelve weeks, 480 hours
Course No.: 98013-01-02

Schuylkill Technology Center
240 Airport Road
Pottsville, PA 17901
www.sttc.ptd.net
Course Name: Class A CDL
Course No.: 00006-01-01

Smith & Solomon School of Tractor Trailer Driving
2011 Woodhaven Road
Philadelphia, PA 19116
www.smithsolomon.com
Course Name: Tractor Trailer (CDL/A) Driver Program
Course No.: 00002-01-01

Trans American Technical Institute
109 Trans American Road
Jermyn, PA 18433
P.O. Box 321
Carbondale, PA 18407
Course Name: Tractor Trailer Driver Training, 240 Hour
Course No.: 80016-01-01

TENNESSEE
M. S. Carriers Professional Driving Academy
1940 East Brooks Road
Memphis, TN 38116
www.mscarriers.com
Course Name: M. S. Carriers Professional Driving Academy
Course No.: 98005-01-01

Tennessee Technology Center at Crump
3070 Highway 64 West
Crump, TN 38327
www.crump.tec.tn.us
Course Name: Truck Driving
Course No.: 99010-01-01

Tennessee Technology Center at Dickson
740 Highway 46
Dickson, TN 37055
www.dickson.tec.tn.us
Course Name: Commercial Truck Driving
Course No.: 99003-01-01

Tennessee Technology Center at Knoxville
1100 Liberty Street
Knoxville, TN 37919
www.knoxville.tec.tn.us
Course Name: Truck Driving
Course No.: 99001-01-01

Tennessee Technology Center at Memphis
550 Alabama Avenue
Memphis, TN 38105
www.memphis.tec.tn.us
Course Name: Truck Driving
Course No.: 99011-01-01

Tennessee Technology Center at Morristown
821 West Louise Avenue
Morristown, TN 37813
www.morristown.tec.tn.us
Course Name: Truck Driving
Course No.: 99002-01-01

Tennessee Technology Center at Nashville
100 White Bridge Road
Nashville, TN 37209
www.nashville.tec.tn.us
Course Name: Truck Driving
Course No.: 99020-01-01

Tennessee Technology Center at Ripley
127 Industrial Drive
Ripley, TN 38063
www.ripley.tec.tn.us
Course Name: Truck Driving
Course No.: 99008-01-01

Tennessee Technology Center at Shelbyville
1405 Madison Street
Shelbyville, TN 37160
www.shelbyville.tec.tn.us
Course Name: Truck Driving
Course No.: 99009-01-01

Transport Training Group, Inc.
P.O. Box 990
White Pine, TN 37890
Course Name: Basic Tractor Trailer Driver
Course No.: 99004-01-01

TEXAS
ATDS-Prairie Hill
P.O. Box 41; Fm 339 S at Highway 84
Prairie Hill, TX 76678
www.truckingschool.com
Course Name: PTD—100
Course No.: 88001-01-01

Houston Community College
Northeast Commercial Truck Driving Center
555 Community College Drive, Building B
Houston, TX 77013
www.hccs.cc.tx.us
Course Name: Six-Week Open Enrollment Class
Course No.: 98018-01-01

WASHINGTON
Bates Technical College
1101 South Yakima Avenue
Tacoma, WA 98405
www.bates.ctc.edu
Course Name: Truck Driver Commercial Local Program
Course No.: 98017-01-01
Course Name: Truck Driver Commercial Long-Haul Program
Course No.: 98017-01-02

Northwest Career Training Center
3707 South Godfrey, Suite 104
Spokane, WA 99224
Course Name: Commercial Drivers License Level 1 Basic Course
Course No.: 98016-01-01

Western Pacific Truck School
9901 Evergreen
Everett, WA 98201
www.wptruckschool.com
Course Name: Advanced Tractor Trailer Operator
   Program—180 hours
Course No.: 98015-04-02

Western Pacific Truck School
11020 South Tacoma Way
Tacoma, WA 98499
www.wptruckschool.com
Course Name: Advanced Tractor Trailer Operator
    Program—180 hours
Course No.: 98015-05-02

WISCONSIN
Fox Valley Technical College
1825 North Bluemound Drive
Appleton, WI 54913
Course Name: Truck Driving
Course No.: 93002-00-01

WYOMING
Sage Technical Services
2368 Oil Drive
Casper, WY 82604
www.sageschools.com
Course Name: TTD—150 Basic
Course No.: 91003-02-01

CANADA
Fifth Wheel Training Institute
P.O. Box 1345
New Liskeard, ON P0J 1P0 Canada
www.5thwheeltraining.com
Course Name: Class A-Z Truck Driver Training Program
Course No.: 00011-01-01

KRTS Transportation Specialists Inc.
23 Industrial Drive
Caledonia, ON N3W 1H8 Canada
www.krway.com
Course Name: Full Program
Course No.: 98011-01-01

Veri Institute of Professional Truck Driving
245 McConnell Street
Exeter, ON N0M 1S3 Canada
www.veritrucking.com
Course Name: Professional AZ Operator
Course No.: 00001-01-01

Top Fifty Trucking Companies

The following carriers of general freight, packages and parcels, heavy equipment, motor vehicles, refrigerated products, household goods, petroleum, auto parts, bulk commodities, hazardous materials, chemicals, and other goods transported by trucks are the fifty largest in the United States and Canada, listed by revenue. This material is reprinted courtesy of Transportation Technical Services in Fredericksburg, Virginia (toll-free 1-888-ONLY-TTS).

United Parcel Service, Inc.
55 Glenlake Parkway NE
Atlanta, GA 30328

Federal Express Corp.
P.O. Box 727
Memphis, TN 38194

Schneider National Carriers, Inc.
P.O. Box 2545
Green Bay, WI 54306

Roadway Express, Inc.
P.O. Box 471
Akron, OH 44309

Yellow Freight System, Inc.
10990 Roe Avenue
Shawnee Mission, KS 66211

Consolidated Freightways Corp.
16400 Southeast CF Way
Vancouver, WA 98683

J.B. Hunt Transport, Inc.
P.O. Box 130
Lowell, AR 72745

FedEx Ground
1000 RPS Drive
Coraopolis, PA 15108

Con-Way Transportation Service
P.O. Box 3301
Portland, OR 97208

Ryder Integrated Logistics, Inc.
3600 Northwest Eighty-second Avenue
Miami, FL 33166

ABF Freight System, Inc.
P.O. Box 10048
Fort Smith, AR 72917

American Freightways, Inc.
P.O. Box 840
Harrison, AR 72602

Overnite Transportation Co.
P.O. Box 1216
Richmond, VA 23218

Swift Transportation Co., Inc.
P.O. Box 29243
Phoenix, AZ 85038

Werner Enterprises, Inc.
P.O. Box 45308
Omaha, NE 68145

New Bern Transport Corp.
50 East Ninety-first Street, Suite 305 A
Indianapolis, IN 46240

USF Holland, Inc.
750 East Fortieth Street
Holland, MI 49423

Watkins Motor Lines, Inc.
P.O. Box 95003
Lakeland, FL 33804

United Van Lines, Inc.One
One United Drive
Fenton, MO 63026

Allied Systems, Ltd.
160 Clairmont Avenue, Suite 600
Decatur, GA 30030

North American Van Lines, Inc.
5001 U.S. Highway 30 West
Fort Wayne, IN 46818

U.S. Xpress, Inc.
4080 Jenkins Road
Chattanooga, TN 37421

M.S. Carriers, Inc.
P.O. Box 30788
Memphis, TN 38130

Estes Express Lines, Inc.
3901 West Broad Street
Richmond, VA 23230

Landstar Ranger, Inc.
P.O. Box 19060
Jacksonville, FL 32245

Quality Carriers, Inc.
3802 Corporex Park Drive
Tampa, FL 33619

Allied Van Lines, Inc.
P.O. Box 4403
Chicago, IL 60680

Averitt Express, Inc.
P.O. Box 3166
Cookeville, TN 38502

Landstar Ranger, Inc.
1655 Inkster Boulevard
Winnipeg, MB R2X 2W7 Canada

TNT Logistics (formerly CTI Logistx)
10407 Centurion Parkway North, Suite 400
Jacksonville, FL 32256

Covenant Transport, Inc.
P.O. Box 22997
Chattanooga, TN 37422

Landstar Inway, Inc.
P.O. Box 7013
Rockford, IL 61125

Prime, Inc.
2740 North Mayfair
Springfield, MO 65803

Old Dominion Freight Line, Inc.
P.O. Box 2006
High Point, NC 27261

Viking Freight, Inc.
6411 Guadalupe Mines Road, #3130
San Jose, CA 95120

Southeastern Freight Lines, Inc.
P.O. Box 1691
Columbia, SC 29202

C.R. England, Inc.
4701 West 2100 South
Salt Lake City, UT 84120

Atlas Van Lines, Inc.
P.O. Box 509
Evansville, IN 47703

A.A.A. Cooper Transportation
P.O. Box 6827
Dothan, AL 36302

CRST International, Inc.
P.O. Box 68
Cedar Rapids, IA 52406

Saia Motor Freight Line, Inc.
P.O. Box A Station 1
Houma, LA 70363

Crete Carrier Corp.
P.O. Box 81228
Lincoln, NE 68501

Rocor International, Inc.
P.O. Box 75367
Oklahoma City, OK 73147

Ruan Transport Corp.
666 Grand Avenue
Des Moines, IA 50309

Quebec Express, Inc.
1890, boul des Sources
Pointe Claire, QC H9R 5B1 Canada

Penske Logistics, Inc.
3401 Enterprise, Suite 200
Beachwood, OH 44122

Central Freight Lines, Inc.
P.O. Box 2638
Waco, TX 76702

Contract Freighters, Inc.
P.O. Box 2547
Joplin, MO 64803

Trimac Transportation Services, Inc.
2100-800 Fifth Avenue SW
P.O. Box 3500
Calgary, AB T2P 2P9 Canada

Mayflower Transit Co.
1 Mayflower Drive
Fenton, MO 63026

About the Authors

Marjorie Eberts and Margaret Gisler have been writing together professionally for twenty-one years. They are prolific freelance authors with more than sixty books in print. This is their twenty-fourth VGM Career Books title. It is also the first career book for which Kevin Crider has provided valuable assistance.

Writing this book was a special pleasure for the authors as it gave them the opportunity to talk to so many road warriors. They also enjoyed riding in eighteen-wheelers and limousines to gain a better understanding of the careers described in this book. The authors especially appreciate the effort that people on the move are putting into making America's highways safer for all drivers.

Marjorie Eberts is a graduate of Stanford University, and Margaret Gisler is a graduate of Ball State University. Both received their specialist degrees in education from Butler University.